the

PERFECT

LOSS

A DIFFERENT KIND *of* HAPPINESS

Printed in the United States of America

05   04   03   02   01   1   2   3   4   5

ISBN: 978-0-9843991-0-9

Cover Design by Mary Hooper/Milkglass Creative
Cover Photo © 2010 — Hooper

the PERFECT *LOSS*

A DIFFERENT KIND *of* HAPPINESS

CHIP DODD

SAGE HILL
RESOURCES
– Feelings Needs Desires Longings Hope –

To
Tennyson *and* William

Write down the revelation

and make it plain on tablets,

so that a herald may run with it.

For the revelation awaits an appointed time;

it speaks of the end,

and will not prove false.

Though it linger, wait for it;

it will certainly come and will not delay.

HABAKKUK 2:2-3

PREFACE

LIFE IS TRAGIC; GOD IS FAITHFUL.

Jesus the Christ has transformed my life from the time of my youth until now, and He will be doing so beyond the publishing of this book of dust. He does so because He wants me, whether I like the action or not. He has kept me a child, so I can remain like he made me: dependent. He has given me a desire to give myself away, so I can have more beyond my self: servant. He has given me a passion to see a vision fulfilled: leader. He has made me a dependent servant leader, an emissary of a great and glorious God.

Jesus said that He came to give us life and that life to the full. Jesus calls us to see who we are made to be, so we can do what we are made to do. He desires for us to live with passion in intimacy with integrity, so that we can live fully, love deeply and lead well. In the Beatitudes, Jesus gave us a declaration of liberty and fulfillment. In eight statements, Jesus gave us keys to the storehouse of life and it to the full. This book is about the storehouse, the quest for our lives and God's unending goodness. And it is about how to live it, beginning with the fact that we cannot do it, but He can.

When I was in my high-school years, I remember seeing the Beatitudes. I actually have memory of my eyes on the page. I just had no idea what they meant. I thought they were something I did with the right attitude and action. At that time in my life, I frequently read the Bible, looking for something I could not find, something I knew I needed and something I tried hard to do. I tried to be good; I even wanted to be good so bad things would not happen. I really did not feel good, though. The Bible, I thought, would (and did) tell me how to do the things that would make me good, so that I would be okay and not afraid. Do these things and be successful—if not really successful, at least somewhat acceptable.

I thought the words were something someone could do, with concerted effort and focus, and then things that were good would happen. I believed life was made up of the following mantras: do to have, perform and reward, action equals results, ultimately, create your own destiny. If you think it, you can achieve it. I didn't know that we do not have such power, as to make destiny, though we do have the power to refuse God's desires for us. Humans work like they have such power. Life does not work like humans demand. Life is actually what occurs while we make our plans. Life is bigger than us. God remains lovingly greater than the life we know and better at planning than our limitations could ever bring us to. He is destiny.

———————

I became insane, no longer whole with myself, others, or God, trying to perform enough to make me okay with myself, others, and God. I believed that I could do enough things that would make life fulfilling and me not afraid. I attempted the impossible with God's help. We humans delude ourselves with this kind of insanity. I had forgotten that God does the impossible without our help. Every child knows that to be true, and when life does not happen like the child imagines, they cry perfect tears and God hears them.

Not until after many years later would I find that the Beatitudes present the doorway into liberty and the pathway into life. When I finally remembered how I was created, I began to see what I had missed and could have restored and much more. I did not just look at the Beatitudes on a page; I was allowed to move into them. And now I have no desire to live anywhere else.

The Beatitudes have been referred to as ascending steps—like order that we climb. Without doubt I see them as steps, but not that we climb. They are more like movements of progression and expansion that God does for us as we surrender. They bring us close to God and to the full harvest of "dirt living" on this earth. They bring us into full life in this world, the tragedy and beauty. They also hand us spiritual eyes of eternal focus and transformative vision of heart.

The Beatitudes, also, have been called circles that concentrically and continuously bring us back to our beginning admission of need. They are. But they are circles like a honeybee's flight, rather than circles made by a compass. The bee's flight without fail is purposeful, pointed and passionate. The flight pattern looks like the flight of the blind, chaotic even, yet it zigzags its way pulled and pushed by scent and sense of the flower and the hive. The bee will do this wonderment that makes food from flowers to its death, serving because it cannot do otherwise, perfectly predesigned. The circles of the Beatitudes are like chaos that has God's mysterious, unfailing order branded to them. They are steps and they are circles, yet we are led through them and shaped by them in a way that will not give us control. He has control; we have freedom and fulfillment.

The Beatitudes are a blessing promise: the statement of a King who came to us as paupers to declare us emissaries, to let us see who we were made to be so we could do what we were made to do.

They declare an invasion of truth into reality, and point to a doorway into a new kingdom. Jesus is a King who has a kingdom, and the Beatitudes are the gateway and then the pathway into the fullness of both, the King and His kingdom.

Finally, the Beatitudes are a mystery, impossible to do; the words are directions to a surrender that sets us free. He does it; we let Him. He reconciles us to ourselves, each other, and Him. Then we, in all walks of life, offer the medicine of recreation to the sick of heart.

This book is not about my life. It is about life, which has me in it, too. From the first page to the last page, it speaks of redemption, recreation, and reconciliation.

the BEATITUDES

Blessed are the poor in spirit,
for theirs is the kingdom of heaven.

Blessed are those who mourn,
for they will be comforted.

Blessed are the meek,
for they will inherit the earth.

Blessed are those who hunger and thirst
for righteousness,
for they will be filled.

Blessed are the merciful,
for they will be shown mercy.

Blessed are the pure in heart,
for they will see God.

Blessed are the peacemakers,
for they will be called sons of God.

Blessed are those who are persecuted because
of righteousness,
for theirs is the kingdom of heaven.

(Matthew 5:3-10)

REMEMBER

I'm not big, but I am a big deal.
I lost the latter and tried to change the former.
Power became my drive, rather than passion
making me fully present.
Power over presence.
I was safe but lost.
Hell is a door locked from the inside.
Jesus said that He came to seek and save what was lost.
I had lost my way. I had lost the truth. I had lost heart.
I was losing my life; the life He came to give.

CHAPTER
ONE

BLESSED ARE THE POOR IN SPIRIT,
FOR THEIRS IS THE KINGDOM OF HEAVEN.

When I was eight years old and in the third grade, I woke up one Sunday morning before others in my family. At the time I was also awake to wanting to be near to God in some way. I don't remember if I dressed first or went first to my parents' bedroom to get my mother to ask her if she would take me to church. She put on her housecoat and drove me down Maymont Drive, out Clark Boulevard to Tennessee Boulevard, and within minutes I was walking up the large set of concrete steps. I barely remember being in the building at all. I do remember leaving the service, stepping into the bright sunlight outside one of the three large white double doors. Mr. Batey greeted me with a white, kind smile and told me I had on a fine-looking tie. He bent at the waist, reaching down to shake my hand as I headed out with everyone else back down eight wide concrete steps.

The church was a traditional building; red brick, white doors, large stained glass windows. The windows, though, were a solid color, not stain-glassed stories because the denomination considered holiness somehow to be about a lack of adornment. They did not understand beauty or loveliness or magnificence or creativity. I guess they figured we would be distracted away from God by creativity.

Down the steps and across the street was the home of the president of Middle Tennessee State College. From that spot home to my house, the street was lined with campus buildings and grass on one side and classic bungalows and homes from the 1940s on the other. Then, the late 50's and early 60's houses started being built as the town grew. Going the other way from the church half a block went to East Main Street, which ran to the square past some of the grandest houses in the world. In the summertime, the sound of cicadas and tree frogs, the aroma of tree leaves, and even the scent of houses decaying were all somehow comforting. It would awaken longings in me that people have when home, summer sounds and smells, like when life's history becomes a nostalgia that we can feel.

The tie I had on was my favorite clip-on, a gold yellow and red paisley worn with my white button-down, short-sleeve shirt, followed by my church pants, and church shoes. Church shoes were hard-soled and dark; shoes you can't run well in.

As I walked on the sidewalk toward home, I remember the shade of mulberry trees covering the sidewalk. The sound of the mulberries that had dropped from the trees popping under my shoes sounded good. I remember shade and sun painting the yards and sidewalk, grackles making their scratchy cawing, and a warm summer morning with just a few clouds in the blue sky. All of the colors were sharp. I liked God a whole lot, maybe even loved Him, felt close to Him, wanted to be with Him. I believed. Somehow I just knew. I went on down Tennessee Boulevard, crossed Clark as Tennessee curved, turned right on Maymont, and walked along the curb to my home. I felt good, just good. It was like that feeling you get when you know somebody likes who you are, so you smile a little, but you're embarrassed all at the same time.

Another time, very close to Christmas Eve, I stepped out of the back seat of our car at home pretty late one night. Time on a clock meant nothing. Dark a long time meant something. Before I went in the house, I looked up at the stars. The sky was covered with them, like cold twinkling lights. One of them must have been very, very bright a long time ago, shining the way for the Wise Men and shepherds. I knew it was so, my heart just knew. And it was also kind of lonely in an okay sort of way.

Every year at my elementary school we had a spaghetti supper, followed by games set up at booths in the gymnasium. We had a ball. It was a fundraiser, which I didn't really think about. I just wanted to buy tickets to do the contest in order to win the trinkets. What a magical celebration. People would bring things from home to donate as prizes or we could win pencils, erasers, or key chains with the school logo. In my opinion, key chains were only meant to be decorations. I did not have keys. My parents had keys.

The duck-floating game with the numbers on the bottom of the ducks caught my eye. On the top shelf were the best prizes. I saw the picture of Jesus, the one in Gethsemane where He looked to God for help, but God wouldn't give it because He wanted to help us through His Son, so He couldn't. I wanted that picture. I knew Jesus was alive still, and I wanted to be near Him. I liked Him a lot. He cared. I could tell by His face. He also hurt. God liked Him, too. I played, and I won the picture.

When we all left the spaghetti supper, my paper sack of prizes in hand, I tripped off the sidewalk just outside the cafeteria and fell into the grass in the dark. My sack landed on the edge of the concrete. I heard glass crack, and I knew it was my picture that I had won from the top shelf. I looked when we got in the car and the crack went three ways; I cried and nobody knew why. The picture disappeared somewhere later. I guessed that they didn't fix glass during that time. The broken glass meant the picture was ruined. I had no idea where I would put it. I just wanted to be near whatever it all meant.

God was like cool green fescue, and He could paint with colors like blue and yellow. He loved the sounds of meadowlarks in spring and fall, rolling thunder, rain, and laughter. He knew the sounds of birds' wings that fly over in flocks and the spicy taste of persimmons. He liked sparrows and pumpkins, our feelings and the sun, baseball and His son. He was crazy about His son; they talked all of the time. God sent Him to tell us all about these things that He liked, and we killed Him for it. I did not understand that part yet. I do now. I'm still sad about it. I'm glad, too.

We all know somewhere in our hearts that life as we know it is not like it was made to be—that there is more to life than the reality we see. Jesus came into this tragedy of survival and brokenness to reconcile our hearts and life to a great God who has greatness for us. He gives us reconciliation, redemption, recreation, restoration, and repair here on earth and final fulfillment and repair later on in heaven. He makes us fully alive to ourselves, to Him, and to others again.

When we get older we forget to believe; we get rid of the heart, subordinating ourselves to survival, rather than living in surrender to God. I did, anyway. And I know someone else who did. I pushed the truth of me, God, and others away and forgot as reality overwhelmed the truth. Reality overcomes the truth until the truth overwhelms us again, if we are blessed by desperation for it again.

There is no way back to childhood, and no one created by God would wish truly to become a child of earth again. There is no way back, but there is a way through to believing fully. We become children of God Who shows us the truth that overwhelms reality every time.

———

As I say, I pushed truth away, and I know someone else who did, too. Actually, I have known hundreds and hundreds who have.

There was a young girl in Israel a long time ago whose heart, dreams, hopes, and hurts were just like every other child. Sometimes in the quiet of the early morning, she saw the sun rise, casting shades and shadows beautifully across her surroundings. She heard the sparrows close to her window. She became excited and frightened in the noise of the marketplace. And during the cold nights of winter, she longed for warmth. She chased whirlwinds that picked up leaves and dust, then watched them spin about and disappear. She hummed a song in her heart of love, hope, and creation, believing life's dreams come true. She hungered for her father's comfort and for her mother's care, and she believed with hope. She cried out in the dark and reached for goodness. She was not ashamed to be in need.

Jesus said of children, "Let the little children come to me, and do not hinder them, for the kingdom of heaven belongs to such as these." (Matthew 19:14) Another time his own disciples asked Jesus, "Who is the greatest in the kingdom of heaven?" (Matthew 18:1) He called a little child and had the child stand among them. And He said, "'I tell you the truth, unless you change and become like little children, you will never enter the kingdom of heaven. Therefore, whoever humbles himself like this child is the greatest in the kingdom of heaven.'" (Matthew 18:2-4)

Jesus spoke of the children, not because they were good, but because they were still living human truth. Children cannot not hide their neediness, their tears, their fears, their joys, and they live in surrender of the possession and expression of their hearts. Jesus calls neediness and reaching out from our neediness faith.

The girl mentioned above also heard and saw things that made her heart slip backwards and close in silent isolation. When her heart went numb to truth, she lost her way, and became everything no child dreams to become. Even her beauty became a doorway to despair and contempt. She became contemptuous of her neediness and she lost the eyes of heart to see the sun's rise and to dream. Shadows and darkness cloaked her. Only clinging memories of hope remained within to cause her pain.

She became an adult. The gospel of Luke calls her "a woman who had lived a sinful life in that town." (Luke 7:37) Jesus will soon call her forgiven and liberated as she crosses the bridge of the first Beatitude.

She learned that Jesus was eating at the Pharisee's house, so she went to Him. What would make her be so foolish and so bold—like a child? Perhaps one day while hanging back on the edge of a crowd or from a window above, she heard this man called Jesus say, "For such as these." He held a child in His arms, declaring life and love for those who could not help but be in need and wish to believe. What if He spoke truth? Or was He himself one more man who left her condemned to pretend and He one more man pretending himself? She had turned her face away from His voice to escape her heart's memories, but she could not escape her hope. When He spoke, she vaguely remembered the sunlit colors of a place she left behind. Even squeezing her eyes shut tightly didn't stop her sight. The flicker of memory, of hope, and of heart drew her to danger, to herself, and to Him.

Jesus had been invited to "the Pharisee's house" for a meal. His name was Simon, but more important was the label—a Pharisee named Simon. A Pharisee had power, position, privilege, and permission. When a Pharisee spoke, either you bowed in subordination, or you could scoff if you were rich and could afford impertinence like the Sadducees. Of course, you could be purely powerful like the Romans and threaten the cross that meant death. The Pharisees were smart enough to play politics with the Romans, despise them and compromise with them, while planning to survive long beyond their absence.

Because they spoke for God, the Pharisees also assumed power over people's hearts, and so could condemn someone long before they ever died. Freedom came from doing enough for God so that He would be temporarily pleased enough to bless you by leaving you alive. The idea of crying out, reaching for mercy, believing in need, tenderness, touch, and grief like "such as these" was the childishness of once being little, but no more. The Pharisees' fear of their own hearts was potent with the power to influence even the stoutest child to doubt God's creation and stifle the hunger pangs to cry out for God to do for them what they could not do.

They spoke for God, but most of the leaders had forgotten their hope in the God who can change things from the inside and be Present with us; they had forgotten the God who said, "The LORD your God is with you, he is mighty to save. He will take great delight in you, he will quiet you with his love, he will rejoice over you with singing." (Zephaniah 3:17) They had too much pride and responsibility to believe the words, "How gracious he will be when you cry for help! As soon as he hears, he will answer you." (Isaiah 30:19) They no longer taught that the heart turning to hope and resting there is salvation nor that in quietness and trust is God giving us strength. (Isaiah 30:15) They would no longer have any of it. So the people paid. The sinful woman had tired of believing, succumbed to power and forgot her heart while they worked to ignore theirs. She had become so tired.

Somewhere beneath her despair, a shred of color and breath like a light whirlwind moved her out of the shadows into the Pharisee's world where Jesus, her destiny, reclined. The Pharisee had invited this Jesus person, someone notable for the time being, to dine with him and others. This was a meal in which Jesus would be assessed for placement and privilege by the distinguished.

In Simon's judgment, Jesus failed miserably, and quickly, because of how he treated this intrusive woman.

She stepped into the midst of the meal, carrying an alabaster jar. Simon knew exactly who she was and previously had "mercifully" avoided his duty of condemnation, because she had never shown herself outside the shadows. He knew she was a sinful woman, and as she stood behind Jesus at his feet, Simon decided Jesus was no prophet, of no import, for he neither rejected her outright, nor ignored her with disdain.

She broke every rule; even the poorest of the poor decently waited until the well-fed left the scene before they came in for the crumbs from the table. She became an affront and essentially asked to be stoned. She had judged herself by stepping into this exposure. It would be her fault.

She had condemned herself, she knew; but she was so tired. Either death or hope, shadows finally covered by darkness, or the flicker of a dim memory was true. Either he truly knew something or death. The last step she could take left her standing behind him at his feet. Words stuck in her throat. She tried to say, wanted to say for "such as these" like a question, but the only sound were tears touching Jesus' feet. Tired, so tired, so lonely, no pride left, only dried, broken hopes. She cried loss, fury at men, hatred of herself, doubts about everything; tears flowed out and fell away like the memories of old promises whispered to her on bird's wings when she was little. She fell to her knees, one last move before death. Either life or death, but at least this much life before I die. Her tears fell. Her neediness, her hardness, her cynicism, her belief, wishes, memories of sunrise and birds and dreams, her knowing smile all faded on to his feet as she wiped his feet with her hair. In the beggar's pose, she began to pour out the perfume, the wages of her work, an offering to Jesus from the darkness of her life. She poured out her whole life upon him, naked creation before Him, with Simon looking at them in judgment. She exhaled the breath of the grieved out; resting at his feet, just there, the hope of a beggar and the hope of creation.

Jesus, give me one or the other because I can not live anymore in the deadness of my life, she may have thought. Quiet all around.

She then heard Jesus speak, not to her yet, but to Simon about Simon himself and his self-righteousness. Jesus told the simplest of stories:

"Two men owed money to a certain money lender. One owed him five hundred denari and the other fifty. Neither of them had the money to pay him back, so he canceled the debts of both. Now which of them loved him more?" (Luke 7:41-42)

Simon replied, smartly, and probably with sniffing indifference and a clear push to end the whole gathering; he knew all he needed to know: "'I suppose the one who had the bigger debt cancelled.'" (Luke 7:43)

Jesus recognized the heart of Simon's words, for he said to Simon, "You have judged correctly", and yet Simon missed every single tear and every movement of neediness. Simon, ironically, had suddenly become the one with the greater debt.

Five hundred denari the woman would never have been able to repay. The amount presented a mountain that the woman could not climb. It was impossible. She knew with everything in her. Simon "supposed" indifferently, but she fell at his feet; Simon looked down at them both.

Then Jesus said, "Do you see this woman?" Simon looked at her. Jesus saw her through the eyes of his heart, and her heart had been poured out at his feet: her heartache, her terror, her sin, her neediness, her loss, her refusal, her hardness, and her small memory of whispered hope of life from a time she had forgotten.

Jesus then spoke to her after creating refuge around her with Him and offering Simon the same opportunity to have what she was receiving: "Your sins are forgiven.... Your faith has saved you. Go in peace." How could this be? Could faith be born in neediness and love be available to the grotesque?

She heard Jesus' words, but did not move. He lifted her chin toward his face. She saw into His depths. The words fell over her like water quenching all of her. She could not capture them; she could only meet them in her heart. The next words frightened her: "Go in peace."

Where would she go? She had already worked herself to deadness looking for life. She found no peace. How could she go in peace if it meant returning to everywhere she had already been?

I think, I believe, that she asked Jesus if she could stay with Him. She had found peace in His Presence, His Voice and His Face, so she would go where peace is—with Him. The doorway to life opens, and she stepped into the quest of life called the kingdom of heaven.

She was once a child, and she remembered. I was once a child, who like her, would work to forget and ignore. I, too, would remember, but not until I became more like her. We are all like her in one way or another. She is everyone who has Christ. She is our human story, and she found the doorway to life through her neediness. Jesus meets us there to take us to life, the life we are made for.

Blessed are the poor in spirit,
for theirs is the kingdom of heaven.

If all the Beatitudes were synthesized to one statement, it would be to exhale to know poor in spirit; inhale to live in gratitude. We crave life like air. Poor in spirit means to be below impoverished, desperate, having no way to go but that of a rescue. It is the absorbed blow of recognition that, "I cannot..., can't...make my own life." Fulfilled or blessed are those who awaken to their neediness and cry out accordingly in their neediness. Jesus said that those who see and feel and surrender to this depth will have God's domain opened to them.

A pauper falls down against a door he cannot open, running from what he cannot defeat. A king opens the door with a lantern in the dark, kneels down beside him and says, "I'm so glad you are here; I have been seeing you. Now, I can be with you." We don't understand what is happening so much as that we know somehow the hope of home has come again.

We step into another place; we see, we feel, we need, we desire, we long and we hope again, and we are met in this place by a King.

"Jesus said to his disciples, 'I tell you the truth, it is hard for a rich man to enter the kingdom of heaven. Again, I tell you, it is easier for a camel to go through the eye of a needle than a rich man to enter the kingdom of heaven.'"

"When the disciples heard this, they were greatly astonished," (which means that their brains were overwhelmed and only the needy vulnerability of their hearts was available). Then they asked the pauper's question, 'Who then can be saved?'"

Jesus looked at them, the true selves of them revealed in their powerlessness, and said, "'With man this is impossible, but with God all things are possible." (Matthew 19:23-26)

The simplest way to put the contrast of opposites is to say that what you have no dynamite, no power to do, God has all the power to do. I would spend a long time building walls of refusal to hide my neediness and to forget my hope before I received the gift of this truth for myself.

CHAPTER
TWO

BLESSED ARE THOSE WHO MOURN,
FOR THEY WILL BE COMFORTED.

Years rolled by, and I grew up. My brothers and sister became like islands in proximity, my mother burdened, and my father troubled. He tried to be with us, but he couldn't. He worked extremely hard as a physician, a surgeon, and he worked extremely hard to make his dreams come true. After leaving behind a double-shovel plow, mules and a place of shame, he moved on to acquire a name, a mission of healing, but unfortunately, no escape from shame. His people did right, had character and knew a world harsh enough to make them expect disaster and fight anyway. They knew rules, lived by them, and missed relationship. They loved, but it was too painful for them to speak, too awful to have and lose. Speaking love became vulnerability, awakened memories, and made them see and know powerlessness— so they stayed in shallow waters, silently and facially urged others to do the same, and then built floodwalls around their hearts. My dad left that thinking behind and still did not escape the power of it because it was in his heart and his mind couldn't fix it. No intellect, no will and no morality can do what only the heart is made to do.

My father had an older brother who became a plant manager, working just as steady and as enduring as a mill grindstone; he became an elder in his church, smiled softly, talked gently, except when triggered, kept quiet. His eyes were not rejecting. My father's oldest brother was in pain; he was highly intelligent, received the foursquare medal in high school and a scholarship to the University of Tennessee, went to war, became terribly diseased as an alcoholic, and died a miserable, yet relieving death at a V.A. halfway house. No one ever spoke the relief. No one even spoke of him again, really. Another memory placed in the region of the forgotten.

My father suffered. His father died in his arms. Pop, my grandfather's name from us, Bill to all who knew him, had heart trouble. My father helped take care of him at the hospital where he went to get checked after having chest pains while working in the garden. Pop wanted to go home after they could find nothing wrong with his heart. He said, and it was known then, that people who went to the hospitals ended up going to die, not to be healed. They always waited too long before they would go, so they blamed it on the hospitals. He wanted to go home, so he would not die.

At the end of the day, my father took him home. It was country dark out where they lived. The only light out there was a security light in a hayfield nearby and a lamp light from the house. They were going to surprise my grandmother with Pop's return. He stepped out of the car. As my father went around the car to help him walk in, Pop dropped to the ground. Dad picked him up in his arms and ran to the front porch, yelling for his mother to open the door. The night is dark; the porch is dark. It's too late; he died of a massive coronary on his own front porch with my father on his knees holding him. He desperately wanted to heal him, heal them, and make the tragedy of life stop just for a while at least for them, just for a while. But a while is never enough when doing the impossible of making tragedy stop. That time never arrives.

His mother finally opened the door and found them. My father felt more shame than ever. He talked less than ever. His smile never lasted after that time, and they were never long before. Christmas came a month later. My grandmother died of cancer a few years later. My father had accomplished many dreams, but the inability to change his insides from the outside, leave the past behind without having to see it and feel it brought the inner pall over everything. Finally, to keep working harder, he began to take the drugs made for help and healing to keep going. But they took him downward to a darkness he had never really left behind inside of him. He became trapped in the dragon of addiction, and his own eyes disappeared into the dragon's poison.

From then on, that magnificent man, who was born in hope and driven by the desire to heal so that he could be okay, remained tormented by his own powerlessness to fix enough. And he was tormented by the impossibility of fixing himself without crying out from deep inside. A heart can only be changed from the inside to the outside, and the change is like a death. The change will cost us everything we cling to that makes us safe in our own power. The price we pay is exceedingly worth it, but I didn't know that for myself until years later.

In 1982, my father was intervened on by colleagues. He went to treatment. He worked it, and he has never stopped working it. In recovery he found the rest of his giftedness, and he proceeded to establish a physician's health program that became an example of aiding the ailing physicians; it even became a prototype for other states. He has since retired. He and I love each other very much. I like being around him; I respect him. He has a brave heart.

I was grown before the healing started, though. Those were silent, scary, numbing times. I didn't know from day to day whether or not my dad would live or if anything would ever be better. By then, though, I needed help. I was on a train track in a boxcar, working to do the impossible, yet destined to go where the tracks go instead. Every single day it was never enough, and every single day summoning the hope to endure again. The past repeated itself. I knew a world harsh enough to expect disaster and fight to endure anyway, while existing in denial of my own self.

I remember when I determined not to cry again, so I wouldn't be a disappointment and could be what I thought I should be. Dad sat in his chair at the kitchen table. I walked into the kitchen from somewhere and was caught by his eyes. He looked at me with disgust on his face and dislike in his eyes, no words. I didn't know what I had done, but it felt like more than something I could be sorry for or fix. It was just me. I froze in my tracks. I stood still looking at the floor. I was afraid. I glanced up; he was still looking at me. My chin quivered, I tried to stop it. Tears came anyway. He looked away out the window, exhaled what sounded like giving up on me. I slid away. "Watch out" became clearer. "Don't show" became a way to stay clear. Power over the weakness of being human became a goal, a way to matter and belong, and then almost a personality.

Belonging and mattering would be achieved through not being who I was made to be. This thing starts us on a course of missing and forgetting our lives—the one we are made to live. Putting our hearts aside to wait for life, while working for a life we cannot find without our hearts fully involved creates insanity. Survival and love make a grotesque couple. Power and presence exist in conflict rather than the integration that makes one powerfully present.

By the time I was a freshman in high school, I believed that I was a disappointment, even a source of disgust to my own father. He did not look at me with delight, or pride, or joy. He did not look at me much at all. When he did, I feared what he thought. I didn't know really that he carried an inner turmoil, his own pain from somewhere else. We, children I mean, are like that, you know. We so want delight from the ones who brought us to the family that we absorb into our permeable hearts their pains as our personal rejections. We so hunger to be loved that we still accept the turmoil as our own because it gives us something to do to maybe make it stop.

Hearts hidden make powerful people with no presence about them. Hearts with open doors make present people who are very empowered. Presence of heart, though, means tears, laughter from within, getting embarrassed, blushing with hurt, anger, pain, questions of all kinds, needs, neediness, dependence, not denial, vulnerability, accepting ourselves as desirous of life, love, fulfillment, the courage to stand in belief, in closeness to others and God. Mainly, presence means staying alive to heart; not separating from who God made. In fact, the word for separation from ourselves as image bearers of God in the New Testament Greek is *"mainomai"*, which translates into maniac or insane. Many children have to hide for seasons of their lives. The full tragedy, though, occurs when the hiding turns into a resignation. The resignation becomes a belief that the protective self is all that exists, except for the fantasy that some day...some day maybe something will change, if I hang on. We have become insane, separated from the true self. If we are good at performing, we might get an alabaster jar of perfume for our work and our shame or a gold watch, or pension, or a building named after us. But it does not make a life. It makes a prostitute of whom God made to live in liberty.

In the ninth grade, then, I went out for football again. Again? I quit in the seventh grade after one day. I wasn't ready. I remember my own sense of weakness, my own judgment upon myself; I remember the face of my father, and the crush inside my chest when he did look at me that day. I knew I didn't have much time left. Darkness was outside his presence. I needed him to approve of me, so I would be okay.

Eighty-eight of us went out for football in the ninth grade. Fifteen of us were left by the time school pictures were taken for the annual. We ran, we fought, we were humiliated "for our own good", and we didn't drink water because it was for the weak. The coach didn't cut anyone; he didn't keep talent. He let anybody stay who was desperate enough for something that made the humiliation unnoticeable or a continuing confirmation of what was already believed. Most of us were already prepared.

I just thought that I would be enough if I could make the team. I made it. I didn't quit. I was part of only fifteen who remained. I remember one afternoon toward the end of another practice midway through the season, the coach brought us all together. I could hear the sound of a flute coming from band practice in the distance. The fifteen of us gathered around the coach. Practice was almost over, and I would have survived another day to become somebody. I had finally begun to feel like one of the few, someone significant by not being like someone less. I remember the music the band played was from the movie *Patton*, referring to courage and strength. I remember how a breeze felt going through the ear holes in my helmet when I suddenly heard the coach call my name, jerking me into reality.

I was not leaning on anyone, nor standing on one leg. Anytime someone leaned on another or bent legs if practice stopped, they were supposed to be hit by somebody or who got leaned on was supposed to fight who leaned.

After I checked my legs quickly, I heard him say, "Boys, a chain is as strong as its weakest link." As soon as I heard the sentence, I had two thoughts, one "oh, no" and the other, "not this time, not me this time." The question then came, "Dodd, who is the weakest link on this team?" I thought for half a second and then said with great false confidence, "Donnie King, sir." Somewhere inside, this time, I couldn't let it be me. I had worked too hard, dreaded too much, given everything I had; the next stop was just no good. So I threw the other guy over the life raft.

It did not work. I really did not think it would. The coach had his answer already. I just needed to fill in the blank to be released. He slowly said, "Dodd," with all the false pitying drag in his voice that he could muster. Somehow that moment collapsed the scaffolding in my construction project, the one on my insides.

Just the word I spoke next, one word, "me," completed everything. The dust settled in the crash, the empty shame bound snickering ended, and we all went home. I understood that I would not be enough, so distrust and distress, and a hardening of heart against disapproval were sealed. I understood. I removed my heart, hid it, even from myself. I had no real use for it; what used to be me made me vulnerable—no more. I would always, every day, have to fight to be worthy or not survive. Period.

When I was nine or ten after school one afternoon, I experienced something I knew to be the truth. But when I gave up and became world tough, really understood how things worked and what I must do to matter, I forgot the truth, fixed my focus, and moved on. I remember the season was fall because the broomsedge was up full, turning red-gold at the top when the sun went down. The sun was warm but not able to make the days hot anymore. I walked out into the open field near some woods behind our house.

The broomsedge came up to my waist. I stopped in the middle of the field and laid down on my back where the green fescue below the broomsedge was still cool, in spite of the warm sun. The tall sedge made a wind block, and I laid there, watching the sky and the sedge move in the breeze. The sky popped with blue. A flock of birds flew over as the cool settled in. I heard their wings, all of them together sweep over. I knew in that moment that God is present and He is good like wind chimes when a breeze barely touches them. He is here and He would be even closer than a reminder and a mystery. I knew for sure.

During the spring of my fourth and fifth grades in elementary school, I sold seed packets from American Seed Company. I would receive an 11-by-6 inch box from the company full of varied possibilities: zinnias, marigolds, cucumbers, squash. Along with the seeds came a catalog of reward choices based upon the number of packets I sold. I would comb through the catalog gifts, wondering what my brothers or sister might like from the choices. One year I won my brother a pocket watch. The next season I got my sister a sleeping bag. I liked the giving. Later, after the seed selling ended, my mother helped me order a Zesta cracker box kite off of the back of a Zesta cracker box for my youngest brother. He and I flew it in a field beside our house. The sky took it up. He ran chasing me as we flew into the wind. I had no idea that I was advertising crackers; I just loved the oddity of a red box staying in the air and that it worked, and the feel of the air and colors, and I loved my little brother.

Somehow, all of those things faded into dim forgetfulness. Something broke in me. I forgot. I put God somewhere, but He knew where. He did not forget.

I read the Bible still, mostly in secret, because I was ashamed of my neediness. I looked for how to live, what to do that was right, to do right and honor God. I read some of it many nights. I knew it had the truth in it. I prayed for God to fix my Dad, make me good and keep me safe, watch over my mother, brothers and sister. God was the last place that I was afraid. Still, with God, I was always kind of sorry. Yet I still remembered what He was really like, though I wasn't like me anymore.

I remember going out to my grandparents' one night. As we walked past Pop's bedroom window along the stepping-stones that led to the back entrance through the milk porch, I saw Pop sitting in a chair by his bed reading the Bible. It was like a movie. I looked from dark into a lighted scene. The curtains were thin white; the lampshade on his bedside table was white with tiny painted flowers on it. The Bible was in his lap. His head was down, both hands holding it. I wanted to know him more, and I wanted to be strong like him. He was known for his strength of character and endurance.

I didn't realize how courageous I had been in childhood because I had heart. I also didn't know how strong I had become by pushing my heart away. I wanted to do good, be somebody, and I wasn't going to be hurt anymore at the same time. So I would use heart as will to be strong. And heart did indeed become willed, the will to accomplish, do, endure, not feel, be tough without anyone knowing I hurt or was even being tough. Will used my heart and then took over.

After football season ended, the next experiences set the course for many, many years. I was almost 6 foot 4 inches tall at 175 pounds of 14 year-old potential, and the basketball coach thought I could fit into his system some day. I was invited to try out. Had he not issued an invitation, I doubt I would have even known of the possibility.

I always liked basketball. The former coach of the Middle Tennessee State College basketball team lived three houses down from our house on Maymont Drive. His son was my age. I used to go down to his house and shoot baskets all of the time, even when he didn't want to shoot. I can't remember ever seeing his father. I remember how hard it was to dribble a ball on clumps of grass and mud before shooting, especially after a rain. Soon after they moved, the folks at the Catholic church directly behind our house set up two goals in their parking lot. Asphalt dribbling was a joy, and they put up chain nets on the rims. When the ball went through the net, it made a chinking noise that was success. I was scared, but I played with the older boys. We were all terrible, but played a lot. Years later, even before I woke up again, I read an essay that said something like, "Anything worth doing is worth doing poorly." The essayist wrote about enjoyment, passion, and love being enough to make an action worth effort rather than achievement, approval, or competition being the standard of value. I understood the essay because it offered me an echoing recognition of what would come to daylight years later. That third grade boy inside of me knew how to do just that, to do something for the joy of it even if he wasn't good at it.

I played basketball on the school team in the eighth grade. So unaccomplished was I that every other game I got to wear a uniform; the other games, the seventh grader my size got to wear it.

I accepted the invitation to be on the basketball team as a freshman in high school, made it, got out of football, and was relieved not to go back. I had proven myself to my father, but I never told him. Actually, I found satisfaction in proving myself to me. I had become almost untouchable. I was free to pursue something that could be what I liked, prove myself to others, and get away from the true pain of what was happening in me and at my home. I would hope in hard work, I would hope in goals, and then I would hope in God. I decided that I would become an All-State basketball player. I would give everything to that, and if I worked hard enough and was a good prayerful person, God would bless me and let me be successful.

My father didn't care much for basketball. At this time, he was beginning to be unable to care much for anything. He was becoming very sick physically, emotionally and spiritually, yet he was still living his work. My sophomore year, the same year Pop died, I was in a bad car wreck. My dad's world was slipping farther and farther from his control. I was crawling to the bathroom after the wreck because I didn't want to bother anyone. My mother had enough worries. My dad was just surviving the throes of his own pain. My father soon fell into what they labeled depression and it was, but the roots were missed. I worked harder by needing less, secretly reading the Bible, and running for basketball.

Man, did I run. I also acted—everywhere. Down inside where I had hidden my heart and refused it at the same time, I was very serious and talked to God apologetically and suspiciously, "God, please. I'm sorry. Thank you. If you'll make me All-State, I'll give you all of the glory." And sometimes when I couldn't pretend anymore, I would pray, "God give me the pain of whatever ails him; I'll take half; I'll take it all, just relieve my dad, God, please." I promised payments, assumed debts, called out for suffering because suffering for anything good seemed like all there was. On the outside I acted carefree, careless, but I was always careful.

I remember a time after basketball practice. I had finished running steps—running, running, running, always running toward the goal and always running from the inside catching up to me, and running from what I knew was true in the third grade.

I was leaning over the rail of the upper balcony in the upper level seating of the gym. Everyone else was gone. I would almost always stay over, doing extra. I thought I was alone. I had forgotten that I was leaning on the rail. I had long gotten my breath back from running the steps. I was thinking hard about my dad. He had not been able to work for a long time, and he was very sick. He just sort of hid out at home. I was afraid of him dying, but I also knew to keep how sick he was a secret from everyone and me, too. Just the way the disease works. I just kept truth a secret.

The coach, a hard man, had walked out on the floor beneath me, and I had not even heard him. I could hardly believe that I hadn't kept up. Before I knew it, he asked me what I was thinking about, catching me completely with myself. I almost told him that I was thinking about my dad, and how he was really sick, that his body shook all the time, and he wanted to die and he told me, and I couldn't stop it, any of it. That I had no idea what was going to happen and I was afraid he was going to die or worse, and I thought I should be able to do something besides need nothing, and I try to pray all of the time, and I always think of this same thing all of the time, and.... But I would have cried and I would have known how out of control I and my family really were and then worse could happen. I could feel all of this like a future happening for sure, if it is released to the air where everything is real; and truth takes life to be lived, so I kept the truth silent.

I opened my mouth and told the coach that I was thinking about tomorrow's game. He walked off, never before or never after asking me a question that mattered about life. The gym was so quiet except for the sound of the coach's shoes leaving the floor and the hum of the lights. I missed a chance.

I scored 26 points in a game one night. It felt like being full and separate all at the same time, freedom like being a gifted child. The next day at the team meeting on the center court after warm-ups, the coach said, I played better than I am. We all laughed, and I went along. There was no sinking, going down very quietly settling in the shadows; my face never flickered. I believed him because I knew that I could work hard but I would never be any good. Yet I could and would keep working. Thirty years later, I found old newspaper clippings of different games that my mother had saved. The score box reported games with me scoring 19, 18, 16 points and so on. I had been good. I never knew how to use the facts as a way to hold on to the truth. The fact of my own heart and the truth that resided in it had become separate and very quiet. I could draw from its well spring of energy but not let the waters flow into my daily life.

My senior year before the district playoffs began, the coach spoke to every senior. He offered his affirmation lines. After the season we would receive our varsity letters and wool jackets—two months before graduation and a month after cold weather had ended. I looked forward to his words. He surely had seen how I had worked, and he didn't know the half of it. Every day of my senior year after practice, I would go to the college campus, run on campus, work out more, shoot and then go home, sometimes getting home after 7:30 or 8:00 in the evening. I remember the damp air in the fall and fog sometimes wrapping around street lamps, and the sound of my breathing as I ran on campus, more sweat pouring, one more workout. I believed that the work would make magic. Stay focused. I never spoke of the extra workouts to anyone. I could talk a bunch and never tell the truth.

The coach had spoken to a couple of seniors, and then he approached me. He told me that he had never had a player work harder in all of his years of coaching, and he didn't know why I wasn't any better. I thanked him. God, it hurt, but I didn't let it bother me. I wondered what was wrong with me, too.

We went into the district playoffs. I prayed so hard. It was the last chance for my dream in any shape or form to come true. Some miracle would happen. We would win and keep winning.

We lost. Three years in a row we lost the first game in the district. All that running, shooting alone, practice after practice, pickup games at the college with college guys, Christmas Eve practice when I would get the key from the coach, all the prayers, the dedication, the trying hard, the discipline, no carbonated beverages, because they supposedly decrease breathing capacity, did nothing. I gave everything. I was fated after all. My dad was right. I was star-crossed, destined by fate itself to turn up losing cards. It wasn't that God didn't care about me so much as that I was just inadequately formed and fairly stupid, and there just wasn't a lot God could do about me. So God just sort of wasn't able to care about me. I didn't have enough. Just like Sisyphus, I was cursed to roll a stone up a mountain to achieve the top, only to have it roll back to the bottom just as success was in sight. That curse was my only answer as a way to endure my fate. Maybe I would get lucky or maybe the gods would forget about me, tired of watching me not make it and not quit.

I could not save my father, I could not help my brothers or sister, I could not make my mother less lonely or burdened, I could not save myself; God was real and that was pretty much it. Nothing really mattered. We are all alone. Period. That's it.

It's weird how a kid can hang a life on something that doesn't seem to really matter, like symbols. To my teammates, it was the end of a season and high school, a very real transition. To me, it was the end of desire.

When the buzzer sounded to end the game, we left the floor of the coliseum down a long ramp into the bowels of the building to the locker room. I leaned into my locker to get my towel, left my head partially inside it against the open door and broke down. I tried not to, but I did not care anymore. The pain of loss and anger rolled up and over me, pain that would become confirmation of inadequacy and secret self-pity later on as I shoved my heart away.

I could not stop crying. Tears came like vomit. My ribs rocked with them. I sat, put a towel over my head, and face toward the floor, crying. I went to the shower and kept crying with water running over my head and face.

Everyone had left. Finally, the tears stopped. I dressed. I walked up the long ramp from underneath the gym floor. All of the sounds of the next game were in full throw. I came up to look at the game, not knowing what else to do. I leaned against the wall and happened to glance up. My eyes caught the attention of a couple of girls in the stands within earshot. "Look at him; he's been crying," one of them said mockingly. I looked at them hard for a second, had nothing in it but resignation, though. Too ashamed, too tired inside, too heavy with something. I turned, went down the ramp, pushed through the shadowy concrete halls to an exit out into the dark, not to return to myself for the next 14 years. I did everything right and everything wrong because I left my heart out of everything. I used it, but didn't show it. Had it, but gave it to no one. I left the last room of my heart that I still lived in, the room with hope in it, turned out the light, locked the door quietly, and stamped "stupid" on the outside.

I left behind dreams, believing, needing, purity, dependence, longings, desire from way inside my heart, feelings, and the God I once knew so well that I could hear Him breathing everywhere. I left behind man's greatest gift, the heart's ability to cry out and be in the Presence of God. I forgot. I took the first steps of miles and miles away from a boy whose heart I used to know, thinking that there was someplace I could go to get away from him. I walked away from me and therefore, from other relationships and God. The only thing I could not really get rid of was the wishing, wishing that life were different. I also couldn't stop remembering that I used to know something that I believed.

I got it. I faced facts, became an adult, and resigned myself to living life on life's terms. I had no idea that resignation in life and acceptance of life are as different as asphalt and birds' wings.

In the end, I figured, it would all mean nothing anyway. I wasn't worth the trouble of really noticing, and I no longer knew how to say or listen to any voice but the one coming out of my mouth, the one that said things my heart did not speak, hear, or really even believe. What good I would do, if any, would be through others succeeding without me getting to go. I was whipped inside, real, real tired.

A college degree, going to Israel, working on a Christian construction crew, pouring concrete, a master's degree, a PhD, alcohol, nicotine, being nice, acting happy, marriage, rage, betrayal, apathy, nothing could fix me, stop the ache of needing within me or make hope stop. It all just made the hope more painful because the belief in it seemed so impossibly far away.

I remember an acquaintance died in a car crash when I was a junior in high school. I would see him in the hall and speak. I was drawn to him in a way because he seemed full of life. I knew his mother, too, better than him, knowing neither of them really well. At the funeral when I saw the mother, she said that her son had always admired me because I had my head on straight and knew where I was headed. I remember half smiling appropriately, nodding, and yet recoiling inside like a cat pushing away from being pulled anywhere. My head inside of me shook, "no, no, no" and a voice trying to speak after the breath has been knocked out tried to say, "I have no idea, none, none at all. I'm just hanging on." I shook my head in ascent, and said, "Thank you; I'm so sorry." And I was. I walked out, and somewhere in that day practiced basketball and ran, running away from myself as much as running to a goal.

After I walked out of the arena, into the dark, time just started rolling without me really in it. What had been a doorway into success by work was now closed. I became more driven, more hidden, and more hopeless, all at the same time. Except for a period of years working for a Christian construction company, I found little value in connecting with God. I tried to hang on, but my heart was gone. I knew the truth in my head, but the truth had not set me free. I found no real value in relationship or work or the Word. I wanted God terribly—needed Him, but couldn't have Him. I knew He was real, but I just stopped the thought there, not letting or knowing how to open my heart. I prayed from a distance, but had no touch. My life was becoming senseless but easily recorded.

I was wherever I was and reactively adapted to whomever I was around, carried by influences without ever really deciding anything; I had no compass of fixed direction but for a vestige of hope within saying, "hang on" and a counter comment, "for what?" "tomorrow?" So, everything went into tomorrow, which I dreaded.

I was an adult. I would be somebody—at least I would fight. I didn't know how powerful fear is when I tried to fight without the anger of hope. Geraniums stored in the cellar in the winter don't grow; they just hang on, missing the sun, knowing nothing but reaching for what light sneaks through the vents to feed the desire to survive. Sisyphus pushes the rock up hill. They just do; the other options are death or neediness, and I did not know they were different.

I found out years later that Peter and Judas didn't know the difference between neediness and death either. Judas and Peter betray Jesus, and their own hearts' hopes, dreams and passions. Judas betrays Jesus by turning him over to the authorities of power who despised Jesus' words of freedom and heart and love. Jesus threatened their grip on the world, and their logic and long-range goals to survive. Peter betrays Jesus by denying knowing him. Peter declares that he had never talked to him, even curses with shouts in denial of even knowing who he was. Peter was the one who openly, boldly, with whole heart told Jesus that he, of all the disciples, would be dependable when crisis came.

Both disciples betray Jesus. One remains willful in his judgment, stays on course even when he sees that he was wrong. The other one in anguish and self contempt runs away. Judas condemns his own need to grieve and condemns himself by hanging himself from a tree. Peter runs home to Galilee to suffer survival, loss, apathy and the pain of unending remorse of wishing that he had not failed whom he had loved. One would reject the humiliation and indignity of neediness. The other would humble himself in neediness for the love of a friend. One would reject grief that comes from hoping, dreaming, desiring, and loss. The other would embrace grief, have his heart and his need of Jesus; he would become the foundation for a living gospel that would change the world. Judas' trail leads to a tragic dead end without life or return. Peter's trail continues to lead us straight to Jesus and everything He offers to those who would need and grieve.

Judas walked out of the last meal he and Jesus would ever have together into the dark never to return. He had cut a deal with the Council; for the price of a slave he sold Jesus to them. With contempt for Jesus' failure, Judas saw more clearly than anyone of the disciples how Jesus was bungling everything, how many times he had missed opportunities for getting into the doorway of power and making moves to overcome. When he saw that he had chosen the wrong fellow to follow as to his own agenda, he made a practical, political move. He absolved the Pharisees of getting their hands bloody. Judas would do the betraying and the accusing. The Pharisees would simply take over.

Then hell was unleashed on Jesus' body and mind and spirit and heart. Judas saw and knew that at the least an innocent man was being tortured, at the most the Messiah had come and was being killed. Matthew 27:4 tells us how Judas tried to get out of it; his part at least. He took the money back. He confessed his betrayal of "innocent blood". "What is that to us?" they replied. "That's your responsibility." Judas threw the money into the temple. Then he went away. He took this sin, his neediness, his broken heart, his tears, his bitterness, his resentment, the teachings of the Pharisees' legalistic condemnation, and the last vestiges of hope, sewed them up tightly in his heart without a cry out. He then choked the potential cry out from his heart by hanging himself. He judged himself instead of crying out for life.

Peter betrayed Jesus and had told Jesus that even if all the others fall away, he would stay. "Even if I have to die with you, I will never disown you." (Matthew 26:35) Peter had no idea that Jesus wanted him to live with him in full heart, not die for him. Jesus hungered for Peter to know who he was made to be and then Whose he was created to become. He wants the same for us.

Peter protested Jesus' statement about what would
occur, the arrest, the death, and especially Peter's own denial
of Jesus. Peter was absolutely willing to die with the Messiah,
so that the goal could be accomplished—the overthrow
of Rome and the renewal of Israel as a great kingdom—
and Peter, a nobody, had been chosen to be a part of it all.
Peter would attempt the impossible, all too willing to die
gloriously as long as the cause of victory would make him be
remembered for bravery.

Peter saw Jesus' arrest, pulled a sword to fight to the
death, proving himself ready to die, just like Peter had said.
Jesus told him to stop, put his sword away. Even then Jesus
attempted to tell him who He was when he said, "Do you
think I cannot call on my Father, and he will at once put at
my disposal more than twelve legions of angels" (Matthew
26:53) to stop this if it were the Will?

Peter followed Jesus, from a distance, not falling away.
He saw him beaten, cursed, accused, spit on, and smashed.
In the meantime, others were asking Peter about looking
familiar to them as one who attended to Jesus in his little
band of believers. Peter finally called curses down upon
his head, screaming at the last, "I don't know the man."
(Matthew 26:72) Just after Peter disowned Jesus the third
time, a rooster crowed, as Jesus had said. Just as the rooster
crowed, Luke says that Jesus turned his head and looked
straight into Peter's face. At that moment what Jesus had
said to Peter pierced through the shock of everything, and
he saw himself, saw his promises echo into emptiness, saw

himself alone, and all his dreams of himself and his Messiah crushed and razed.

After seeing, he turned away, stumbled out into the dark and wept bitterly. Shock and despair, then drifting and resignation took the place his dreams once filled. Even the most amazing part of all was that he, a nobody from Galilee, had been special, had a part in something special and had followed the one who had seen it in him. All finished. Nothing left but his own contempt for and foolishness in belief. He went home, back to Galilee and did the only thing he knew; back to survival by fishing. He took the rest of his unfinished tears to the water. He would mourn over a lifetime by himself in quiet moments like he had once wondered, before meeting Jesus, what life was about. Otherwise, he would let no one know him again. He would keep his heart's sorrow and hope well-hidden behind a veil of resignation and despair, but no longer would he use boldness as a tool to proclaim himself. Who would believe him anyway? Peter went home and simply tried to settle in to all the loss, but for that memory of his love for the Man and the journey they had lived.

The story doesn't end in Peter's grief or in his attempt to resign himself into forgetting as best he could. At Jesus' tomb, Mary Magdalene, the one who had nowhere else to go but to the place she knew Jesus' body would be and Mary, Jesus' mother, and Salome found that the stone had been rolled away. When they entered the tomb, "they saw a young man dressed in a white robe sitting on the right side and they were alarmed. The man said, 'You are looking for Jesus the Nazarene, who was crucified. He has risen! He is not here…But go tell the disciples and Peter. He is going ahead of you into Galilee. There you will see him, just as he told you.'" (Mark 15:6-7)

"Peter," the man said, "Peter." The one who more than anyone, had talked the biggest, said the most, promised the best, and ran the farthest. Peter, the one who Jesus called the rock, a natural leader, the neediest, most impulsive fellow, the one who loved and hated, the one who had betrayed, wept, and run had been named specifically in a message from God: "Don't forget Peter. Remember Peter"—as if to say, he hurts so terribly, he doesn't believe he can ever believe again. Sometimes he has trouble breathing, carrying his body around, so heavy with sadness without end. Tell Peter that Jesus will meet him in the place he went to disappear. Jesus will meet him in the last flicker of hope he can not rid himself of, the same hope he had as a boy who could wonder the impossible on moonbeams that reached across the surface of Galilee's waters. Hope in the person of Jesus and the Spirit was coming to Peter if he would let his heart be seen.

They were fishing when Jesus showed up on the shore of the Sea of Galilee. He called out to them about the night's catch, which had been poor. I wonder how much their concentration was on fishing anyway. They did as the stranger said and sent the nets across the boat, making a net straining catch. John said, "It is the Lord!" (John 21:7)

Peter heard him, threw down his self-condemnation and resignation. He quit deciding for God and instead threw himself toward God. In his excitement and desire, he threw himself overboard to swim to his Messiah. He stood on the shore dripping, returned to help with the net, then came back to Jesus again. The Master had appeared. The servant's heart needed him desperately. Jesus asked Peter if he loved Him. "Yes, Lord, you know that I love you," Peter replied. (John 21:16) *3x Peter denied*
Now - 3 times Peter confesses

Three times Jesus asked, three times Peter confessed his neediness of heart and love. The betrayal, the sin, the contempt disappeared like a whisper into a thousand canyons—gone. Peter remembered God had said that He remembers we are made of dust, that our sin will be separated from us as far as the east is from the west.

The God of the seven hundredth and seventy-seventh chance was already present as Peter presented himself. Peter found comfort, the freedom of yielding, and a passion for his personal Savior. Peter also found deep humility and comfort beyond anything he had ever conceived. Blessed are those who mourn loss, dashed dreams, crushing blows, wasted times, endings, pride and self destruction, darkness, the rejection of ourselves, for they will know the surrounding Presence of God and the miracle of others' care. Peter, for the rest of his life, would never be alone, even when he was with himself only, for God's arms were there. He knew the God who tends his flock like a shepherd; He gathers the lambs in His arms and carries them close to His heart.

Some years later out of his own experience with God, Peter would write the following tender words and deliver a clear alert to all of us: Cast all of your concerns, every one on Him because He cares for you. Let your whole heart be placed in God's mighty hands that He may lift you up. God opposes those whose hearts are in refusal, the proud, but gives grace to the humble, those in need. Attend to your daily lives with care and know your need of God, for "your enemy the devil prowls around like a roaring lion looking for someone to devour." Remember that you are not alone. Everyone who knows God's closeness is experiencing the same struggles. (I Peter 5:5-9)

Lions hunt for the stragglers, those who leave, the lame. Put in human terms, the enemy prowls about looking for those whose hearts are isolated from their own admission of neediness and their own pain of loss. Peter knew life from the inside out, knew the Savior's touch, and followed the presence of Him until his own last breath. The One whose care he had received, he couldn't leave.

Blessed are those who mourn,
for they will be comforted.

The English language does not express the full relational, gentle graciousness of this Beatitude. The first Beatitude speaks to the depth of our powerlessness and the pain of being able to feel eternity within us. After we face our failure and our pain, the process takes us to seeing and feeling the truth of our lives. Peter faced his powerlessness and pain. He mourned and knew the intimacy of finding security in his neediness before the Presence of God.

Blessed are those who mourn when they see what their rejection of neediness has cost them, others, and God. And fulfilled are those who have faced their lives, know their hunger and feel their pathos, the pain of living and their need for they will be heard and called by name, invited into security, wrapped in wings and upheld by Spirit. The Beatitude is a promise of security and comfort, and the birthing of God being intimately involved in our lives. God sees our destruction and moves upon our outcry as a creation site. He brings the oil of hope into the broken recognition of our grief. He cares for us in the midst of the damage we cause protecting our selves from pain.

The pauper is lifted up, and then introduced to home. Arms of care hold them, and a voice says you can rest now, "I am here and I will not leave. You're here with me; we will do the rest together from now on."

I did not yet know such mourning, nor such comfort as Peter received. I had begun to walk Judas' path. Years would pass before I would have the great, good fortune to have my own grief.

CHAPTER
THREE

BLESSED ARE THE MEEK,
FOR THEY WILL INHERIT THE EARTH.

A part of this story that continues to unfold to this very day is my life with Sonya. We met in high school, dated seriously off and on, then on, married, stayed married and now love each other like we were made to when we met. Early on when I met her I was drawn to her, truly smitten actually—in a way I had hoped to experience one day and in a way I had no capacity to grasp because the attraction was forever.

I was sixteen and Sonya was fifteen the first time we went out. As the fourth quarter horn went off at a Friday night football game, I had positioned myself to be standing beside her with my prepared statement about going out the next night, to a friend's hayride. I told her that we could go to a hayride together—all cool—and I would pick her up at six—all cocky—like "surely you will cancel anything else you could possibly be doing because I have picked you."

I remember what she was wearing that night—green and white patterned cardigan with metal buttons, green pants and flat bottomed brown laced shoes. Her hair was curled at the bottom and her cheeks had some blush from the cool night air. Her eyes were (still are) olive and jade green with light sparkles in them; they were green pools of mystery and depths to a goofy, romantic child heart who caught a glimpse of something good when he saw her eyes.

When I was young, a bunch of kids all around the same age would play hide and seek at our house until the mothers would end the game around nine thirty on summer nights. All children were safe except for the limits in the darkness of night on the four edges where we knew not to go. Home base was like the touchstone where we would all be together again safe in the light. Home safe. The one who had been picked as "it" to count to one hundred while everyone else hid would be alone wandering in the dark to catch someone, and the others would all be relieved and laughing if we weren't "it". If someone didn't come in on time, or showed how good he could hide too long, we would worry about the stranger in the dark, maybe the "Thing" had gotten them. We would yell "ollie-ollie-umph-frump-free" to signal the game over so the person would run in to home base. We would get on them and tell them about the "Thing" or tell them they weren't so cool, or tell them we thought the "Thing" had gotten them. We had all seen *Creature from the*

Black Lagoon, so everyone knew what the "Thing" could be. Sometimes the game would drift into story telling about monsters, or "did-you-see" followed by whatever someone was saying.

One night I hid in the thick bushes on the side of our house. I belly crawled on the grass through a small opening in the front of the bushes into a small room-like area just big enough for one person. As the sounds of the game and the summer night echoed around me, I looked up through the branches of the bushes into the dark sky and noticed how bright the half moon was; I could see stars flashing like little diamonds on a backdrop.

I knew something that I could not understand. I knew that I would grow up someday, and that my life was out there away from this summer night. A future of hope and dreams filled with life was out there in the moonbeams and diamonds where God lived. I was scared and filled with wonder, and I was sad and thrilled to be where I was when the "it" walked by the bushes without seeing me.

I jumped out after "it" passed and ran to home base fast as lightning, laughing loudly as the person behind me couldn't catch up. After the game I remember liking everyone very much, remembering everyone clearly because I knew it would end. I wanted both—the future of wonder and the present full of life. In that moment I had them, and it was really good and sad.

When I looked into Sonya's eyes that night at the football game, pretending like I knew what I was doing all cool, I glimpsed what I saw in the bushes that night. The present and the future—hide and go seek on a summer night and moonbeam lights cast upon a path of believing in more.

The glimpse was it, though. I had already left behind much of what I knew. I wish the story from that point onward could be idyllic, the way we long to have life, but instead God's faithfulness so often shows most clearly through tragedy. The same way the beauty, the richness, and the detail of a photograph is taken from the negative.

So much of life is like this pattern—tragedy, then redemption to victory—because we rejected God's freedom in the beginning, initiating tragedy. Freedom seems like such a wonderful thing, but only if we recognize it as a gift and treat it accordingly. The responsibility of freedom humans have failed miserably. We take the gift and use it over and over and over again to refuse how we are made for relationship with our own hearts, the hearts of others, and the heart of God. Instead of finding full life in how God made us, we use our freedom to refuse relationship if it costs us potential pain of hurt or more hurt; we block with fierceness the very thing that can grant full life—a vulnerable heart before a good God.

We initiated the tragedy of life; we chose independence from Him rather than dependence upon Him. God has never stopped pursuing us though. We initiated destruction by rejecting how we are made and thus Who made us. I needed liberation from the tyranny of my own over-whelming, defensive ego so I could live fully dependent upon God again like when I was young and like I was made to do as a man—young or old.

Not until years later would liberation come, when in my neediness I would finally surrender to God's longstanding, ever present goodness, so I could give out of my true heart to Sonya what her heart had clung to believing could be.

I pursued her the only way I knew to do and keep myself from getting hurt more.

I would see her, speak, then ignore her. I would acknowledge, offer something of attention, niceness, then withdraw. I was nice and mean, confusing and threatening. She knew the love in her very being that she had dreamed of, and I set about to destroy the very experience she and I were made to have. My false person would do so much to keep my true self from any vulnerability.

Sonya gave me a loving card after we had dated for a short while that had a rhinoceros on the front and a statement on the inside I can't remember. What I do remember is that she signed, "I love you" with a small heart drawn just above her name. I was amazed, shut it quickly and was afraid of something. It knocked upon the door of the place I had sealed shut and boarded up. Some time later she asked for one of my senior pictures in the hallway. I told her that I would be glad to sell her one. She walked away quickly. I thought I was being funny. Cruelty is never funny, nor is withholding love, or being defensive. I took her vulnerability and smashed it like I smashed my own. I loved her inside my heart but could not let my insides come outside but for moments before my pride, my expectations related to fears I couldn't admit, and because of the shame, the deep confusing belief that if she really knew me, she would find me deficient, turn her face away in disgust or even worse in pitying kindness and walk away, leaving me the sniffling fool.

The creature from the black lagoon had me, dragging me away from the boundaries of summer nights. I could see moonbeams and stars and home base. She called out "ollie-ollie-umph-frump-free" and I couldn't run home. "It" had me.

I was defiantly opposed to being in need and yet loved her in my heart. I would tell her that I didn't love her, that we were just friends. We were too young to be in love. We needed to date other people. After I started college, she was still in high school, so it was immature for me to date a high school girl. I criticized her, left her guessing, would say mean things until she had had enough, then I would feel shame, be nice, or make promises. It took her a long time to say, "Enough, no more." Love would just have to die or win.

Whenever I saw her I was in conflict, and whenever I was with her she was at emotional risk in my conflict, too. I loved her best away from her when the defenses weren't mantled all around me. She would tell me years later that she could love me most freely when I didn't know she was watching. She could catch me being the person I feared she would reject. Therein lies tragedy. I didn't believe the truth about love enough to risk seeing it. And I could only remember enough about it to react against it for fear I would love and be hurt.

So, I introduced Sonya to my family secrets and demanded she deny them, too, just like me. My Dad was very sick with a crisis-filled addiction and severe depression when I met Sonya. We called it overworked, dedicated surgeon. My mother was overwhelmed by everything she couldn't control and the lead pretender. We called her carefree and fun loving. The four kids filled our slots as needed to keep the snarling hunchbacked disease way in the background, so we wouldn't have to see it defecating in the middle of the table, showing us its latest masterpiece during every single family meal.

The way the monster wants to isolate us from love astounds me still. In isolation we can be destroyed more easily. The good meals were the ones when Dad wasn't there; we would laugh and be outrageous and hurt each other's feelings. The best meals were when my brothers and I would make French fries and hot dogs and watch *Magnum PI* or *M.A.S.H.* before we would go our separate ways or to bed. "Normal" meant staying away from the truth. In our case, it was the centrifugal force of doing whatever to avoid the hunchback. The family would have to spin apart while leaving dead weight false selves who could pretend that all is well.

For Sonya to fit in with me, she had to play a part in acting like everything was okay. She needed to support the partial and occasional truths as the whole story, the gospel of a happy family.

After all, my father did overwork, as most surgeons do, my mother was a lighthearted person, we did like hot dogs and French fries. My sister was the only girl, so she had the right to be moody and spend lots of time alone reading about England. That was what girls do. We laughed like crazy and said horrid, funny things because we were carefree. We were quiet around the doctor out of respect. This was my good news and it kept us all safe, and Sonya needed to grasp her part.

For Sonya to be safe with me, she would need to cooperate in the same denial I found my safety in. So I introduced her into the inner workings of addiction, beginning with what you think you see, you don't. What you think you feel—you don't. What you think you need—you don't. And ending with "if you think you're going to talk about anything except for what is prescribed—you're not," that is if you want to belong or matter in this group anyway.

Denial permits survival if addiction has control, addiction to anything from alcohol to work. Addiction thrives like cancer unchecked through denial, and denial is as good as life gets for everyone involved. Don't see, don't feel, don't need, don't talk about what really goes on within you, including imagining yourself free to live fully. And don't trust that anything is going to change if you do see, feel, need, or talk in the truth. Denial is the breeding ground of addiction, the stagnant water, environment for mosquitoes, the beginning of malaria, the initiation of death. Addiction, too, is so much bigger than alcohol and drugs. The work addict doesn't say on his deathbed, "I wish I had spent more time at the office." He bemoans, if he has any courage, the abandonment of his family. The control addict abandons the heart of their children because control means power over others' hearts. Addiction ultimately is the set of behaviors that take us away from facing that we are made to live dependent upon relationship with God, others and how we are made. Full life is in this dependency. Addiction deludes us into believing otherwise. Anyone who runs from heart is addicted to something. Evil uses addiction to keep us away from life to the full because that life will attract others to liberation, then Evil would be vanquished.

Therein lies tragedy. I did not believe the truth about love enough to see it and trust it. And I could remember only enough about it to be damaging, rejecting love because it was childish, thus shameful.

Addiction works this way. It takes love that is a gift, turns it on its head, and then says you receive all things for performance. It also takes the God-given gift of child dependency that God uses to make us heroes of faith, and it calls this dependency foolish and stupid. God's ways become an abomination to man-made thinking. Thus, addiction comes right out of Evil's toolbox. It is the bottom-line result of independence from how we are made to live.

Like many of us, we keep secrets we don't really know we have because we fight to stay away from the place we store them.

By the way, I am not blaming my Dad or my Mom. I am not blaming their parents, or their parents, or their parents. I am, however, not excusing any of us. I am saying what every child knows: if the emperor has on no clothes, well, he has on no clothes. The child of denial grows up to either act in to keep his heart closed, remaining forever immature or to act out on everything around them to make the world change, remaining likewise forever immature.

Sonya begged me with tears not to go to my house, but I would take her there anyway. She had to be part of the pretending, so I could get permission to love her. If they didn't accept her, I would have to go against them, and that would expose heart, and heart couldn't be exposed because that meant being out of control and that would create more problems, which would make feelings exposed and that would be vulnerability and vulnerability was close to the truth and the truth went against denial, direct opposition, in fact, and if denial were breached, then all kinds of terrible things could happen worse than how good things already were, so...things just needed to remain the same.

While all of these inner workings were going on, I also would run over to her house in the afternoons, sometimes carrying some small flowers in the pocket of my sweathood. I would make things for her, romance her in my heart alone. Later on, I made her a cedar trunk while she taught school in South America. I brought her shells, an ancient oil lamp, and clothing from Israel when I returned from an archeological dig in Israel. I wrote letters of love from the wheat harvest in the Midwest. I bought her pearls, gave her a bird nest shaped like a heart that I found in a small tree when I was bush hogging. I built her a desk made from discarded wood on a construction site where I worked building condominiums. The top of the desk was an inlay of the sun coming up over a mountain range. The desk was so big I had to pull it up over the balcony of her parents' house to get it into her room where she was living for a time during college. It wouldn't fit through a downstairs door. I did not think to measure.

On and on the list goes, but my actions remained confusing. I would not risk living love with all of its mess out loud with her.

Sonya and I dated off and on for nine years. She remained sexually and spiritually pure with me as I truly wanted to do with her. But she did it; I worked against her purity. I attempted to feed off of her purity and her believing and her child-like faith, and I hoped somewhere inside that she could survive where I was headed.

Sometime during the college-age years, I'm not sure exactly when, I had a dream about daybreak, and I awakened sobbing. In the dream, I saw Sonya from the inside out like who she really is as made by God, a child and magnificently loved. The fearfully, marvelously and wonderfully made, knitted together in her mother's womb, woven together in the depths of the earth from Psalm 139 is who I saw. Sonya. I saw her, woman-child full of wonder and grace. I saw her with the eyes of my heart, the heart God shaped and I saw my own condition. And I spoke to no one about it.

I had walked up some steps from a basement of an old ivy laced college classroom building that had tall stately, stone columns, white trimmed windows and burnt reddish brown bricks. The steps led from inside the building to the outdoors and up to level ground. When I was high enough up the steps to see ground level, I looked upon a flat plain of grass, stately buildings in the distance, and trees with leaves that were like poplars. The grass had light coming from it and luminescence reached out from the ends of leaves from huge trees. Life extended from everything. Out on the grass to my right, some distance away was Sonya. A couple of cameras, a pair of binoculars, a monoscope, and a small telescope looped around her neck. She was seeing and receiving everything around her calmly, deeply, peacefully, seriously and joyfully as she stood in the canvas of creation about her. She had on a white cotton smock with light colored flowers and turtles and rabbits imprinted on it, like a nursery blanket design or a young girl's precious dress; she had on jeans and wore flat tennis shoes made of canvas with wide white shoestrings.

She had just put one of the cameras or the pair of binoculars back on her chest when she suddenly did a cartwheel. I remember being stumped in an amazed way when the pile of research and wonder equipment didn't clobber her in the head. It all dropped toward the ground and followed the circle she turned the cartwheel in, all landing back where it was, untangled, and without hitting her.

She saw me and walked toward me, a slight smile, natural, no surprise to see me like no surprise to turn a cartwheel with cameras around her neck, or no surprise that everything sprang out with light. Kneeling down at the edge of the grass by the steps, she said, "Come with me," very kindly, softly, and without questions. Come with me—all invitation—natural like a child simply expecting to ride the tail of a comet to the moon, not wanting me to miss it with her. I remember saying, "I can't," and the moment I did my feet began to descend again back to earth, to the basement. She looked at me, with only the slightest question in her face when I did not move. Inertia brought me back to reality; I began to awaken; I was sobbing. Never before and never since, have I awakened in such tears. I saw Sonya's inner self, who she is, the one I loved and the one I tried to change into someone I could control, to bind her to the earth instead of blessing her by knowing her for who she is and Whose she is.

The dream was truthful. Not until years and years later could I love her like she was God's, not mine. People are not ours. They are their own, unless they don't have God, too. If they don't, they try to own or be owned. God loves liberty, for its very sake. He set us free in Christ. I saw Sonya set free, woman-child full of wonder and grace. I could not enter that world, nor could she live if she descended into mine.

I had no words for what I had seen, nor faith, nor ears to pay attention. I just had a dim, dim memory of a place I had never been. I knew that I loved her.

A few years after we started dating Sonya gave me a present she had made for me—for no reason but love. It was a colored pencil drawing of a character called Ziggy who was holding an umbrella under which stood a cadre of different animals, all smiling in the company of each other not in the rain anymore except for one duck that clearly enjoyed the water. The comic figure Ziggy was a pure presentation of love and care in spite of all of life's travails and struggles. He simply wouldn't quit loving, and was unable to do life any other way anyway. He found beauty where others saw waste. The caption that she drew said, "Love One Another." Sonya sketched and then colored the drawing and pictured her heart for me and her wish for me and for her. For all the human foibles, struggles, the travesties, ugliness, her image bearing of God within her wanted nothing but something so simple that even a child has no hesitation of hoping in it and no hesitation of doing hope at all. That simple love was all that Sonya wanted, and to this day remains life fulfillment to her.

Sonya and I married a year after my father returned from a very successful, extended treatment for addiction. He had become who I once had thought he would be. He was my best man in our wedding. He was giving and joyous at our wedding. My mother didn't feel good the day I got married. She told me that she didn't think she would make it, but she would try. Thankfully, she made it.

I cried silently when Sonya and I kneeled together to listen to a man with a solid voice sing the "Lord's Prayer" acapella at the very back of the church. Tears ran down my face as the truth echoed from far away. My dad told me later that he wished he had thought to have a handkerchief. I loved even the thought because I'd never been able to hear such gentle words come from him until that day. He had spoken them before, but all I could hear and see was what I heard and saw.

There is a picture in a scene I remember when the photographer took pictures after the ceremony ended. Sonya looked up into my face like the photographer posed her and I was looking back at her in the picture. She loved me with an oceanic quietness and depth, and she loved me with a simple, faithful heart. I smiled into her eyes in that picture, and I remember wishing that she would not look at me that way, uncovered, clear, pure: she lived her wedding day. I essentially missed it. Her eyes looked for me and I could hardly tolerate that much care and love. It was too open. It would draw me out; I wished that she would not be so open. Years later, I would give anything to see her eyes again.

Seven years later at a church we attended, the pastor called for us to turn to the person beside us to sing a benediction. The benediction went like this: "May the Lord keep you, may the Lord bless you, may the Lord make his eyes to shine upon you." Sonya would look me in the eyes then, too. I could not hold her gaze of hope and tenderness and now pain. I was too ashamed to look at love, now a love after seven years that I still could not deserve. The marriage was a slow separation from her love, my blame for her inadequacies that I concocted out of my own fears, and my looking for worth, a worth that she couldn't give me. I began to seek approval in all of the wrong places, and gave myself to the influence of others who I became like. I went to the bottom.

Before I began the descent to the bottom, there was a small window of opportunity that I refused to let my heart enter. Sonya and I had been married for about six months. We lived in an 800-square-foot barracks-like apartment in Oxford, Mississippi. I had already lived in Oxford for a year working on my Master's degree in English, of all things, and Sonya joined me to work on her Master's in Reading.

We were finally living together after all of those years of waiting. I could see with my eyes how blessed we were. Sonya made our place beautiful. We had plants and prints and photographs. She brought her unvanquished hope to my poverty, made her home and wished for me to be in it. We even created a garden in our backyard, bringing compost from the barn at my parents' place to make a small garden in the backyard. We grew tomato plants that ended up being nine feet tall with no tomatoes. The nitrogen in the compost and the sandy soil overloaded the plants. I remember that she and I laughed about them and we enjoyed each other. She worked so hard to make our marriage live.

I remember one morning she squealed and screamed from the bathroom, "Help, help, help," she said, "a spider." I came in and squished a giant wolf spider running from us as fast as possible. I laughed and enjoyed her need of me. In the wintertime icicles would collect at the bottom of the windowsills inside the apartment. When the heat would click off, I could hear, not just feel, cold air sliding back in from every cracked doorway and window separation that it could possibly come through.

———

I studied literature. Sonya studied giftedness in the education department. I criticized her. Sonya felt criticized. I worked to catch up, to accomplish, to overcome my shame. Sonya invited me to live with her. I stayed up late working. Sonya slept alone. I demanded that she grow up and face how life really is. Sonya began to let dreams slip back into a chest of hope that she had brought forward. I worked harder and left her more isolated. I demanded that she meet more of my needs that I didn't even speak. I taught her how to feel failed as a wife. And I learned how not to even be a husband. I was becoming more miserable with myself. And she was facing life alone.

Sonya and I had returned from our hometown to Oxford, Mississippi, after a Christmas break. My father had been in recovery for two Christmases. I was getting our presents out of a box at our apartment in the small hallway. I unrolled an inexpensive poster that my father had picked out for me, had picked out one for each one of us. Mine showed a kitten hanging from a limb by its front paws and its head peering over the branch, like one last desperate chin-up. The caption read "Hang in there." When I got the poster out, looked at it and recognized that he had picked it out for me, I also recognized all of the years that I had not gotten to be with him and the wishes that I could make myself enough to be worthy of his love. I recognized that he had picked something out for me and I remembered all of the Christmases that I had missed with him. I began to cry hard as I knelt by the box of presents in our bare hallway.

Sonya came to me and said, "What, what?" And I said, "He picked this out for me." I could imagine him going to a store, and I could see him think of what would fit for me, mean something to me, encourage me, and he picked it out. I clung to this hope through an inexpensive poster with my broken heart, and I wished I could have my childhood back somehow to know him, so I wouldn't have screwed it up so badly. I felt loved and sad and broken and relieved and alone and grateful all at once. My dad loved me, wanted good for me with my name on it. I was gone and didn't know how to live blessed, my heart was in hundreds of pieces in a room with a door cracked open. I could breathe with a chunk of grief. I couldn't let anyone close to me and yet at that moment Sonya was close to me, and I was grateful.

A heart imprisoned by the will of refusal survives on the deluded hope that I can save myself if I just make myself strong enough. The vow, the will and the determination become the tragedy. Refusal of neediness, dependency, feelings, vulnerability, others' help, the refusal to accept how we are predesigned to need God and others harms everything God has made and intends for us. The liberated have cried out, faced the need and received a rescue. Those who have cried out in tragedy have found the God who is faithful.

Life is tragic and God is faithful. Some of us Christians and non-Christians never get to experience this full dependability of God because the doorways of our hearts are never opened. We live our lives in our brains, figuring

figuring —instead of feeling, fantasizing instead of facing our lives. Our brains are of little use unless our hearts are fully involved. A man cannot save himself. The disciples said, "Then who can be saved?" Jesus said, "With man this is impossible, but with God all things are possible." (Matthew 19:25-26)

Sonya married the man crying on his knees; not the shielded, hard man, but the live-hearted, true one. The true one crouched on his knees in a hallway of a $169 a month apartment, wishing for his dad to tell him everything was going to work, that he was made right, because by God I would "hang in there" until maybe something changed. He knew I was persistent. She married the man that broken hearted boy was made to grow into, but I could not claim him for long for fear of mockery. I was not ever going to be the weakest link on a chain. I would not let down for long. This event and those tears didn't change anything, but what I was made to be like was revealed to me, and I remembered a moment.

I didn't really believe in the ones who said they knew God. They seemed to have no life. I definitely didn't believe in the ones who did not know God, but I did fit better with them because there seemed to be more of life's realities. I, who had once had a standard, began to slip away from really any standards, while pretending that I was still true. I knew how to act.

I wasn't liking myself as the years rolled by, but I was still just filling in. Now we lived in Texas, where Sonya taught school and I pursued a degree in Counseling. I binge drank whenever I was where it was available. I betrayed and broke her heart, not caring for her as I had promised. I resented her and saw her love as inadequate. And based upon what I was expecting, her love was inadequate. I was looking for her to do for me what I couldn't even admit I needed. I was looking for her to do something for me that only God could do in the fellowship of other people. She did not leave me physically; in spite of all of my withdrawal from her, she had just enough to make it through the day with scraps of hope for both of us.

Emotionally, however, she pulled away inside to a safer place. She stayed at school longer, became Teacher of the Year at her school, loved her children, and was adored by parents. She worked more, volunteered more, always away to endure her own loneliness. A lot of women survive, I came to find out later, in this way with men who will not be men.

Finally, Sonya told me one day that she would not live like we were living. She would not live with a husband or a man who wouldn't be one. Steadfast she could be, but a liar playing a part she would not be. She told me that she would leave soon, but she didn't know when. She didn't know where she would go, but she knew that she would not go with me.

I remember sitting in the green upholstered chair in the first house we ever lived in, not looking at her when she said what she said. I sat numb and somehow grateful. I understood somewhere inside where memories of whispered true self and God still talked easily that I was hearing something really, really kind and good and lovely and true and praiseworthy.

I was a bit surprised to hear Sonya say these words because I had changed in my behaviors so much by this time. I had been sober from alcohol and left behind the people I hung with. I had matured, and put work in the place of all the foolishness I had been a part of. I had gotten therapy help and group help, seeing finally the twistedness of getting a degree in counseling when I so desperately needed emotional and spiritual healing. I was living truthfully in word and deed, becoming somebody I could respect. Even then, I was still not emotionally present.

"O, God," I prayed inside, "how do I become the man I so want to be, the one I once saw but cannot find? How do I become the man Sonya knows she can give her heart to? O, God, tell me what to do; I'll do it." My poor prayer God would answer, even though my prayer was still about performance and control, as if I had the power to make myself whole. God will work with any prayer. I did not yet know that God Himself would make me whole. He did not need my help.

When Sonya and I finally moved into our first home, she was so excited. We remodeled, painted, wallpapered together without a divorce, planted flowers and grass and once more she planted seeds of hope and dreams, as did I. Our first son, Tennyson, was born soon afterward. Sonya had left teaching, which she loved dearly, for a deeper calling, to be with Tennyson.

I wanted her to see how much better everything was. She didn't want provision. She didn't want to settle, pretend, and survive. She wanted me. She wanted her. She wanted us. She wanted us with our son, eventually our two sons. William was born two years later.

I didn't have a clue. I just knew that I wanted what she wanted. Yet I was still powerless over trying to get what I wanted through credit seeking for being good. And I was still criticizing her for not seeing how good I had become! Glory be to God who continues pursuit of the clueless, the pretenders, the boring, the deceitful, the insufferable, the "nice guys", the phonies, the stupid, the ignorant and the cruel. Who is this God who will not stop loving and calling us to more life with Him, others and ourselves? I had finally become good again, working hard, being persevering, being tenacious, running hard. Just like when I was in high school, pushing for the All-State goal. "Go at it again," essentially was my most sophisticated form of becoming anything or doing anything. Even though I will ultimately fail—my inside voice would say because I really am defective and unlovable—at least I would fail trying. Perseverance to me meant not stopping for help while I get the unending task finished: superhero. I had no idea that perseverance meant continuing on because I knew that my hero would never be defeated. Jesus had conquered and would leave no one who called out behind. He would come get me.

———

65

Looking back to that day, I wish that I could have been like George Bailey in the movie, *It's a Wonderful Life*. He stands on the bridge at a moment of clarity and powerlessness, seeing that he is in need, hungers for his life, and cries out, "O God, I want to live again, please, God." God does for George, at the moment after his surrender, what he could not do for himself. I was willing, but in my willingness to change, I took back over and just tried harder. Still, I was willing, but willingness that leads to reapplication of determination would certainly take me back to the same place. O, Sisyphus, let go. Fall to your knees. Not yet. Insight did not set me free.

David, the King, above all else knew two things deeply and well—though he ran from both truths several times— as do we all who know. He knew who he was and Whose he was. Much of David's heart or inner story, is spoken in the Psalms, which speak to all of us who are looking for the life in living and know the author of it. David defines who he is and Whose he is in the middle of Psalm 8. David blesses us all with humility and dignity in that Psalm. He looks about the skies at night, seeing into the midst of the vast universe of star upon star as he stands upon the plains of his own beloved land. In the recognition of how deep and wide and unfathomable creation and his Creator are he says,

When I consider your heavens, the work of your fingers, the moon and the stars, which you have set in place, what is man that you are mindful of him,

the son of man that you care for him?
(Psalm 8:3-4)

The question from his insides is followed by a reply that still makes me put my hands down by my side and turn my palms up to ask, "How?"

The answer to David's question is:
You (God) made him (me) a little lower than the heavenly beings and crowned him with glory and honor. (Psalm 8:5)

God says and meek David says that I am not big, but I am a big deal; you and I are not big, but you and I are a big deal. I am made to walk in dignity as a human being, in appreciation of God's creativity and gifts in making me. He crowns me with thick luminescence and substance and giftedness and gifts when I recognize and see that I am only a man. I am man, dependent upon the Creator for life's breaths and opportunity. He made me great in His eyes, and in His eyes I needed to find my self.

But I had left what little I knew of God and had forgotten, pushed aside, the one who was created to remember him. In shame and fear, contempt and resignation, defiance and despair, walking into darkness, I had left God. I had walked away from the place at the table he had set for me and did not look backward to see the light always glowing from the front porch. I walked away from experiencing His Presence, and in doing so, left behind life's aliveness, mission, purpose, passion and greatness—my inheritance. He had done for me what I would never be able to do for me—ever.

I did not believe in His touch. He, however, still believed in me. And he also believes in you, not who we are so much as who we are made to be.

David knew the label of shame, yet because of God, never wore it internally—even when Samuel, the prophet, came to pick the king from Jesse's sons. All the sons presented themselves before Samuel, but David. No one thought to even call him. Not big enough. The Spirit in Samuel did not testify before any of the logical choices. Samuel asked if Jesse had any other sons, for he had been told not to consider his appearance or his height, for God does not choose based upon appearance. God chooses differently. "Man looks at the outward appearance, but the LORD looks at the heart." (I Samuel 16:7) You know, the heart, the substance children have to work so hard to hide, and we forget we ever had in the first place.

When David was called to appear, he had left his job of tending the sheep, the place from which he possibly wrote the Psalm of man's humility. He was anointed king and then returned to the sheep, I assume patiently waiting upon God, and being prepared for the summons.

Some time later David is described to King Saul, the king who precedes David, and who would become his sworn enemy. David "is a son of Jesse of Bethlehem who knows how to play the harp. He is a man of heart and a warrior. He speaks well and is a fine-looking man. And the LORD is with him." (I Samuel 16:18) The LORD was with a man of heart.

In the valley of Elah, the shepherd-king, David, appears again (I Samuel 17). He knows who he is and Whose he is. Goliath stood before the army of Israel, making the taunts that sliver through the cracks in our bravado, grabbing our shame and fears of not being big enough. Fresh from the quiet pastures where he can hear God speak, free from the clanging cymbals of continuous distraction that block the voice of our hearts, David speaks a living truth straight from Psalm 8.

I know my size but that does not equate to my place in God's eyes. He essentially says: Who are you warriors of Israel to let the Philistines speak taunts to our God, the God of Israel? Take heart (show up) be of courage (remember who and Whose you are), stand up dependent on Him, He will go ahead of us. Stand up as He has made you and step out as He has called you. I know of what I speak, for the lion and the bear that would kill my sheep I have already killed in God's Presence.

Let no one lose heart on account of the Philistine;
your servant will go and fight him. (I Samuel 17:32)

The Lord who delivers me from other harm will deliver this shadow of death over to me also. David said that after I kill you Goliath all those gathered here will know that it is not by "sword or spear that the LORD saves; for the battle is the LORD's and he will give all of you into our hands" (v. 47). David's meekness—the surrender of his heart and the submission of his being to the Creator God allowed God to fulfill the Psalm. He crowned David, the human being with glory and honor—God's glory and honor. Blessed are the meek, for they will inherit the earth.

David's dependence upon the Maker of men let him inherit the earth. He went on to be trusted by others and blessed by God to make Israel into a great kingdom.

However, when he forgot his God, his blessings, his heart, and left his meekness behind, harm came to David and those He loved. When he ran from who he was made to be—a little lower than heavenly beings to be crowned with glory and honor—havoc came, even to the point of having one of his own loyal warriors murdered in the battlefields after David betrayed him in an affair with his own warrior's wife.

"At the time of year when kings go off to war," (2 Samuel 11:1), David stayed home, isolated from who he was made to be, isolated in heart from others and from God. David became anxious, as do we all when we run from fear, need and trust. He went to his rooftop, unable to sleep, restless, and discontent. Instead of looking into the heavens and speaking to his God, he looked across the way, and found a replacement for God and his own neediness. Lust always takes the place of love when we attempt to get away from our inner selves. Instead of a cry out in need, David decided to create his own relief, and the most ancient story of mankind repeats itself. No longer a servant, no longer dependent, David shook off who he served in meekness, the One from whom he inherited the earth. He declared himself independent from his own heart and rejected Whose he was. A harmed woman and a murdered friend later, Nathan the prophet comes to David to confront him and love him, to bring grace to the guilty and another opportunity for him to return to humility so he could find his greatness again. David did not deserve it. None of us do. He had destroyed a family, refused God and rejected who he was made to be. He had earned condemnation. But, Nathan brought him the opportunity of mercy born in grace.

Nathan exposes David's secrets and lies, tells him of the consequences that will be in David's family and then makes the most extraordinary statement. He said look at all the LORD has bestowed upon you, and then "if all this had been too little, I would have given you even more." (2 Samuel 12:8)

"I would have given you even more." You went to your rooftop, but did not look for me. You did not tell me where you were or lay your heart before me. Yet, God takes care of those who are His. He does so in detail. We are His through surrender. Surrender literally means give back over. God desires for us to give back what we took from Him in the beginning, our true selves, our wills and our lives. As a man thinks in his heart, so is the man. If we think against how we are made, we die, missing our lives and then we are buried. If we surrender to how we are made to Him, we live and experience blessing that carries on after we are gone. Surrender begins and continues with the giving over our hearts to the One who made them. After Nathan's visit, David surrendered his heart, the feelings, needs, desires, longings, hope of his heart again. His humility brought him back to who he was made to be and what he was made to do.

❧

Blessed are the meek,
for they will inherit the earth.

Usually, our surrender movements don't begin until we are desperate. In our surrender, though, we find Him who we have refused because of our distrust and lust for power. When we are rescued, if we will be, the truth of life begins in our lives. We step into a quest, that we live in His presence and that one day ends in His arms. We will see in His face the love He has always had for us—like with David. "Don't you know," Nathan said, "He would have given even more had you but surrendered your heart to Him who desires you."

Meekness grows through gratitude and desire. The gratitude comes from seeing the rescue we have received. Meekness is born in desperation that becomes gratitude, which creates humility. We wish to be with the One who rescues us; even more we have the hunger to serve, and go with the One who has made life and is good. Meekness, then, becomes the awareness of how much we matter to Him, not because we are big, but because we are "big deals." We cannot fix ourselves; we must be healed by Him. He sets us free to receive. Our willingness to cry out to the One who receives us in our desperation (Blessed are the poor in spirit), and comforts us in our wounds (Blessed are those who mourn), makes us available to receive His gifts (Blessed are the meek). We will receive if we will receive. And we will receive even more if having met Him, we pay heed with our eyes and ears and have our movements based on what He says to us. For He wants and desires and longs for our good. Our surrender yields who we are to who He is. My heart wants to be with Him. By yielding or giving way to Him, we end up in a yield or bounty with Him: we inherit the earth. We yield to yield. We give way and receive His bounty.

The LORD is righteous in all his ways and loving toward all he has made. The LORD is near to all who call on him, to all who call on him in truth. He fulfills the desires of those who fear him; He hears their cry and saves them. (Psalm 145:17-19)

Those who delight in Him, He gives them the desire of their hearts. (Psalm 37:4)

The LORD is compassionate and gracious...He does not treat us as our sins deserve or repay us according to our to our iniquities. For as high as the heavens are above the earth, so great is his love

for those who fear him. As far as the east is from
the west, so far has he removed our transgressions
from us. As a father has compassion on his
children, so the LORD has compassion on those
who fear him. For he knows how we are formed,
he remembers that we are dust... (Psalm 103:8-17)

Fear Him means to know at depth the need of Him and
out of gratitude and awe to be dependent on Him. To fear
is to say in heart, "Who or even what could be so good and
love me so much?"—awe and gratitude. Awe and gratitude
are results. They come from the surrender of failure, loss,
and powerlessness.

I desired to stay with the God I could not live without
and Who could not stop loving me. I began to look for His
love and believe in the possibilities that maybe God could do
for me what I obviously could not do for myself. Though I
did not see yet, I wondered. God was walking me through
the Beatitudes, and I did not even see yet. I wanted to live,
I wanted to love, I wanted to lead. I had the want to, yet I
didn't know how to need without needing being a shameful,
convulsive experience that led to more disgrace.

I had become hungry and could not find the meal
I smelled.

I knew that I needed...something...something,
but what?

I prayed like David after his downfall with Bathsheba,
his confrontation by Nathan, and his reforming by God:

Have mercy on me, O God, according to your unfailing love; according to your great compassion blot out my transgressions. Wash away all my iniquity and cleanse me from my sin.... (Psalm 51:1-2)

Surely you desire truth in the inner parts; you teach me wisdom in the inmost place. Cleanse me with hyssop, and I will be clean; wash me, and I will be whiter than snow. Let me hear joy and gladness; let the bones you have crushed rejoice. Hide your face from my sins and blot out all my iniquities. Create in me a pure heart, O God, and renew a steadfast spirit within me.... (Psalm 51:6-10)

You do not delight in sacrifice or I would bring it; you do not take pleasure in burnt offerings. The sacrifices of God are a broken spirit; a broken and contrite heart, O God, you will not despise. (Psalm 51:16-17)

God wants us and forms who we are from the inside out. He wants our hearts for our good, so He can crown His creation with honor and glory. I knew that I wanted life, and I was discovering that I and my hard work were not the answer. I still did not know what David knew. God was pursuing me, though. Sonya was loving me, too. And I knew I needed a life I could not create.

CHAPTER
FOUR

BLESSED ARE THOSE WHO HUNGER
AND THIRST FOR RIGHTEOUSNESS,
FOR THEY WILL BE FILLED.

Life is tragic and God is faithful. I did not know that life is so much about living it fully and facing how much He wants us and how He has been faithful to give paths of light, creation, hope, and courage to draw us, save us, redeem and restore us. The paths lead us out of the tragedy of darkness, destruction, despair, and death. Life is tragic and God is faithful. Tragedy cannot vanquish the hope He has created within us while we still breathe. It is hope that makes us cry out in the tragedy. It is hope that makes us step out into the invisible where He catches us and brings us to Him. It is hope that calls us to hunger and thirst for Him everyday.

More than most of us realize, we use defiance, resignation, compromise, and isolation to imprison the vulnerability of our hope amidst the tragedies of life. For hope makes us

---

vulnerable. Defiance opposes any hope that renders us vulnerable to needing others or God. Resignation blocks hope and need from affecting our hearts, by risking or believing little. Compromise leads us to use others and God to cut deals to only have some of life instead of openly declaring how much we wish for or need. And isolation pushes us to do anything to keep our selves from being exposed as needy, dependent, trusting, hope-filled creatures.

These four forms of refusal of our hearts' truths eventually imprison us because they keep us from life and love. What begins as protective eventually seduces us into the territory of darkness, destruction, despair, and death. How coy is evil for it befriends first before it poisons us slowly. Only surrender of our hope to God lets Him liberate us. Our claim of control, conversely, eventually leaves us in the void where evil, like a thousand leeches, sucks life's hope from our hearts. He came to give us life fully, to let us love deeply and lead well a life that blesses others.

I could sense the love in my life, but could not see it, like the scent of an approaching rain. Thirsty, yet blind, I could not see to find the water. I was close, but my heart was behind walls of refusal.

I also began to hear things that moved me toward water. I had blindly begun the degree to learn how to help others while in deep denial about how much I needed help. Maybe if I learn how to help others, that will fix me. I had applied, naively, to the University of North Texas, later discovering that it was one of the top-rated counseling programs in the country. I shake my head in embarrassment, with wonder and gratitude at how God marvelously guides with grace which He provides to anyone seeking life, no matter how messed up with pride, grandiosity, shame, impaired thinking thinking, wounds, harms done, sin and denial. If there exists the slightest crack of wishing, God moves in. Always present, He is.

While at North Texas, I took an addictions course off campus, separate from my degree. I heard and learned about adult children of alcoholics. I began to look into how to help "those people." Soon, I began to recognize myself in need. In addition to my classic academic career, I fell into a set of coursework that would through relationship and time change my life. I was in need, I was at a loss, I was willing, and I was desiring to have the life beyond what Chip could make, a love deeper than I could merit, and a vision greater than my own appearance. God, please fully introduce me into who you are, my fumbling prayer remained.

The course content covered alcohol and drug counseling training. The person God put in my path was a woman named Kathy Golla. She had been in recovery and out of treatment for four years. She was striking in the way that she talked. She said something in a small group about "praise God" and then after another sentence or two she said "praise God" again. I recall that she was wearing an athletic sweat suit, a string of pearls, and her hair was red and overdone. I was drawn to her energy, even smiled about her. I also remember being terribly cynical and pitying toward her about her naïve, rather embarrassing, God comments. What a courageous freedom though! I wished good for her and knew that over time she would mature, eventually calm down, and not be so hopeful and certain once she understood how life really works. My fear of believing and hoping rendered me so judgmental.

Little did I know. Golla, I would find out some years later, was a friend of Tom Landry, post-treatment; he was legendary in the annals of professional football and the Dallas Cowboys. She had been closely involved in high-profile interventions, and the story goes on and on. Before treatment, she was absorbed in the luxury of all that Dallas wealth brings. Kathy had finally wound up living in consuming darkness and despair that had brought her near death. The grace of God came into her darkness because of her cry out. The darkness was overwhelmed by light; the despair was overcome by unflinching hope. She praised God because she knew the difference between no God and God. She will need to tell that part herself. Hers is a story of tragedy to triumph through the grace of God, the love of God, and the love of other people who also know this God. She has remained this alive for over twenty-five years.

In my smallness, in my "without God", defiant, resigned, compromising, isolative, intelligent, objective foolishness, I judged her. Even so, her words about God touched me deeply, beckoning memories I kept hidden in a secret place, but could not fully see. I was hungry and thirsty and praying, but I was still so scared to be fully known.

I had very little interaction with her beyond that initial meeting, except for a conversation here and there. I had no idea that this woman who openly praised God had on some level recognized that God could possibly do for me what He had done for her. She saw through my act, past my despair, and into God's desire for me.

Two or three years went by. I continued making my own way, based on my own plans. One day, out of the blue, I received a phone call from Golla. She said, "I have been following your counseling education career, Chip, and I know about some of the help you have given to others. I'm now the director of a multiple addictions unit in a local treatment hospital. Would you come and teach and counsel codependency and the disease of addiction?"

My life had begun to reshape itself over the few years prior to that phone call. I had worked hard to be good and to become good at what I believed I was sort of made to do. I had begun my own recovery from the disease of addiction that I had and grew up in. I had lived the impact of addiction, secrets, denial, shame, loss, resilience, family systems, emotional impact, psychodynamics, and insanity. I also knew that our solution was not better thinking or positive thinking leading to good outcomes. Solution occurred in spiritual ways, with full emotional participation. I knew this in a general way, enough at least to move away from my own power and my thinking being the answer. The human answer had to do with heart, and everything else would follow. That territory is where God works. I knew, somehow, it was a heart matter, but I just could not yet see specifically what I knew in general.

Golla hired me, having seen something in me I did not see. I still believed that if you knew me, you would be disappointed enough to turn away and probably walk away, or worse, stay and judge daily. Sonya still lived with that man. She had said that she could get just close enough to me to run into a black wall of stone. I would find a way to criticize her for whatever she came up with about me. I just reacted against the very thing I hungered for. The cost of admitting that maybe a lot of wealth lay behind a wall was too high because it could be a mistake. I did not want to lose her so I would block her continuous love. That black wall was one side of a black box that had within it almost everything I needed to live freely. Tragically, I was keeping what makes life worth it from her and me—for what? To be in control and to be safe. I was convinced I was not loveable. I was acting properly, sober-minded, and hardworking, but not free to love or be loved.

Turns out, Golla had chosen smartly. I brought what I had gathered so far to the work. I used my own story, my solid education, and my hope for change. Others were getting well while I continued to hope for more. I truly began to see what could be as I watched Golla plow into the "unknown" over and over again, believing that good was coming because God was present and working, whether anyone saw Him at the moment or not. I had never seen such courage. I continued to watch for her to get a grasp of the realities of psychological structures and mature. Instead, she still continued to believe and praise God. She just wouldn't "grow up". It had been many years by this time since she had completed treatment. She continued on, bringing the sacred to the secular, meeting people at their point of need. She imposed nothing on others, but rather, she exposed others to themselves and to redemption. She and I worked together more and more and she believed in me.

I continued to wonder when I would be discovered as a fraud and thrown out by her. Yet I continued to be drawn irresistibly toward that "foolishness" and "too muchness" and her simple God belief. She wouldn't get over it. I did not believe so much in "God with me", but I truly had begun to believe in "God with her". I did not realize that what I was believing in was the Spirit of God within Kathy and her surrender to the Spirit and my deep craving to live near that same Spirit. I did not dare yet believe that I could have that much God; though I could, at least, be around the idea of someone else having God.

Years and years before this time, I had spent several months on an archaeological dig in Israel. We worked in Caesarea, an ancient Israeli and Roman post on the Mediterranean that was a gateway into the Middle East. As the sun would come up, our crew would meticulously dig down toward the ancient of days. We would stop in the early afternoon because of the heat. I recall leaving the site, looking out over the deep blue Mediterranean only yards from our dig. I remember the breeze blowing across us and seeing the present and past converge everywhere: the Crusader fort, Arab pottery artifacts, Roman mosaic work and pottery, coins, and the rich work of ancient Israel. On the beach near where we stayed, artifacts were as common as sand. I remember two white marble columns jutting out of the sand four to five feet high, leaning sideways, indicating a glory that had long since faded into oblivion, except for the stone. During one of our weekend journeys away from the dig, I stood at the Sea of Galilee, near the place where Jesus spoke the sermon that will not fade away.

We were being led by a professor who had a mountainous intellect, and was a kind and true pursuer of God. He was a world renowned archaeologist. He had once been very kind to me after one of his classes during the spring semester. I had followed him out of the ancient history class, seeking his approval. I was talking about a Greek playwright named Aristaphanes, and I wanted to subtly let him know that I had spent extra time at the library reading the Greek plays and unassigned readings to get a better knowledge of the course of study. I mentioned Aristaphanes and Greek satire two or three times during class. He quietly told me after class outside his office that Aristaphanes, which I was pronouncing like "windowpanes," is actually pronounced Aris-ta-pha-nes, as in "bend your knees." In my craving to earn approval, I had butchered the name of this playwright. It was as if I had asked for more hors d'oeuvres by saying "horse-de-voors" at a Harvard orientation gathering. I pissed in my pants on stage.

I had in earnestness shamed myself, and he, in care and integrity, had kindly helped me. That moment was one of the first times I had not experienced absolute contempt inside myself for having messed up so badly. I lived that afraid all the time.

Looking back later, I realized that I had been reading so much on the side without ever talking to anyone about what I read, I read things phonetically only. I had never heard anyone say the names themselves. So it was really a beautiful thing I did in ignorant sincerity, and he did a beautiful thing likewise by caring for me; even more beautiful was my acceptance of that care. That began a relationship of respect, me toward him, that continues to this day.

So while we were standing there at the place where Jesus delivered the Sermon on the Mount, our professor finished pointing out the hill formations near the Sea of Galilee, and how they made a natural amphitheater that probably allowed Jesus' words to be heard from a good distance. He talked about how storms can sweep upon the sea without any warning, and how the sea feeds the Jordan River, but finally dies out in the Dead Sea. How it goes from drinking water, fishing for life and abundance, and then flows away from life to death, ending in the Dead Sea. The Dead Sea is so full of salt nothing can live in it. It appears to be good water, but it is not.

A shrine gazebo had been built to mark the sight where Jesus spoke the words that are a fountainhead of living water. After the professor finished sharing, I moved toward the gazebo. Underneath the roof of the open, airy place, a small group of nuns stood quietly facing the sea. With a voice that floated on the breeze, one of them had begun to sing the Beatitudes. I heard the words, "Blessed are the poor in spirit, for theirs is the kingdom of heaven," then looked out toward the Sea of Galilee in the distance. I took in the breath of what I heard and saw, walked a few steps down the hill, and began to cry really hard. I listened from an unnoticeable spot, to every last note in the midst of inescapable tenderness, and I drank it in. We left that place, I sealed the opening of my heart without even knowing it, and forgot what I would someday remember. I guess I thought the experience was just an event. I did not know that our lives are mosaic poetry —a masterpiece of God being written as we live this life. If we will live this life. I did not know that God wanted me.

Kathy and I continued to work together, and I continued to learn about passion and trust. She would not get over the God stuff. She was dependent upon God, her experiences, the amazing grace of where she had been and where she had arrived, then lastly her certification. I was dependent upon a PhD, academic thinking, appearance, control, and then God. She trusted God, having given up on her power to fix herself. I trusted me, having given up on God to really do anything specific, especially with me.

the PERFECT LOSS

She thought highly of me; I really could not understand why. I overheard her one time in a conversation with a psychiatrist discussing how my skills and talents could be used in the company that ran the hospital. She said, "Chip Dodd could not be bought; he has too much character." I felt ashamed. I figured I had fooled her with my presentation, and somehow she had not seen the "for sale" sign on my back. I loved the concept, though, of being someone like she described. I did have a vague memory of someone like that, but he was a child.

As matters evolved, someone notable in her world asked her to consider beginning a Christian counseling center, to bring the best there is to people in need. She described the conversation as we charted the patients of the day. I sort of presumed that she was talking about me helping her start the place and working with her. Even though I saw that she had not grown out of the God stuff, had not "matured intellectually," she also had not stopped believing and being consistent and being someone of stellar character who had a past of devastation. She lived from the inside out, and believed what she said. Years later, I would read the following words and think of her:

He turned to me and heard my cry, He lifted me out of the slimy pit, out of the mud and mire; he set my feet on a rock and gave me a firm place to stand. He put a new song in my mouth, a hymn of praise to our God. (Psalm 40:1-3)

I believed that I was better with her; in fact, I believed that her God liked her. I knew she was not just lucky. So if a Christian counseling center was next, then I was in. How preposterous, really. I saw myself as saved and lost at the same time. Maybe saved in the end eternally, but lost here on earth. I was also more tired of pretending than I even knew. Little did I know at the time, that even these realities and struggles would later benefit others. I was also homesick for what she spoke about: hopelessness to hope, being met at my point of need, exposed to and then experiencing God, rather than imposed upon again. I wanted to believe, but I wouldn't unless it was real. I was so scared to believe that I kept the truth away from me. I had convinced myself that a general sense of malaise within me was not only normal, but perhaps a condition of the mature or knowledgeable.

While harvesting wheat in the Midwest, I remember seeing a feed lot crammed with cattle awaiting slaughter. They were fed well, monitored for benefit, and then dead. I recall a hill in the midst of the herd. Without pushing or shoving, one of the herd would stand on top of a dried dung hill, catching whatever breeze might blow in the Midwestern summer heat. I thought life on its own terms meant being able to appreciate the breeze when the time came to be on top of the dung hill. The mature found solace and strength in resigning themselves to that realistic scenario.

After I said, "Sounds good," about the counseling center rather casually, still pretending, she took one of those breaths that every ballplayer dreads hearing. He already knows what's coming; the only thing missing are the words "good luck."

She said, "I'm not sure I want you to do this with me if I do it, Chip." I studiously pretended to listen, had practiced for years, and I was prepared to hear. I could feel myself falling quietly, not even surprised. "You're one of the best therapists I have ever met. You're brilliant. You're tough. You're a good man," she continued. I could hear what she was saying, though I could also hear the weighty silent "but." She had discovered me. The weakest link in the chain. I made the team, but I wouldn't play much. Here is the kid who tried hard but would wear the extra uniform sharing it with another player. Here was Sisyphus having rolled the rock up the hill, knowing full well it was going down again—again. I was grateful this time to know my course. I was preparing to start over at the bottom where I knew what to do. Push up.

I remembered the fog on the MTSU campus as I ran at night underneath street lamps and trees dripping with rain after practice my senior year—when I would go run more in an effort to become All-State. The fog was slipping around me and I almost couldn't see. Working hard, hiding heart, and waiting for change by hanging on weren't enough, and never would be. Sisyphus was the pride of mankind, not even brave. "Chip, you're standing up on the outside," I heard Golla say, "but you're sitting down on the inside. What do you really stand for?"

I had nothing to say. Verbal blubber wouldn't work, and for the moment I could care less. In my mind, I could see me sitting with a pen in my hand mid-sentence in the chart, wondering what he did stand for, too. She left the chart room to go home. Soon afterward so did I. Before she stepped out of the room, she told me about a book that she recommended I read called *No Wonder They Call Him Savior* by some guy named Max Lucado. The next time I saw her, she gave me the book, and I truly appreciated her care. But I expected little from the book.

I told Sonya that night what Kathy had said. She concurred with many things that she had said—the good, the great, and the "needs much improvement" part. I was the one who could not see, therefore, I could not believe. She saw in Kathy her own hope for herself and me. Sonya had seen something happening in me after I began to work with her. She saw her prayers on some deep level being answered, hopefully. Sonya saw that this woman was bringing life to me and maybe would bring life to us. In some ways, and it's true to this day, Sonya has so given me to God that she wishes to be second to Him with me, and that's the greatest form of love one person can offer another. I always thought it was rejection. Being second to God in everything with everyone is a great place to be; any other place is an attempt to be God or do life without relationship with God. I was attempting to do both, and wound up a spectator in life. Evil is wily, cunning, and baffling. If it can just influence us to be first or third, we are sidelined for life—never experiencing intimacy and having no fulfillment, on the one hand, or never feeling valuable and having no place, on the other hand.

"Where are you, Chip?" was Golla's question. That question is also the first question God ever asked humanity. He asked it of his first creation in Genesis. "Where are you?" (Genesis 3:9) God asked this after his first people attempted to hide from themselves, each other, and their Lover.

Where was I? What did I stand for inside? This question led to all the other questions. What did I believe? What matters to my heart? What made my life worth action? What would I risk my heart on or give my heart to from the inside out and all the way beyond? What could I see? Where was my heart; for where it was, my courage was also there, as was my faith, my fear, my passion and my anger, my caring and my sadness, my intimacies and dreams and my loneliness, my freedom and my guilt, my humility and my neediness, my healing and my hurt, the joy missed and the image bearing of God Himself. In me were my desire, my longings, the very memory of being made to live fully. And there was hope, precious, painful hope wanting to be freed and attached to something other than survival.

I read the book. I read a book about The Man. The one who wasn't for sale. I met The Man: Jesus, Savior and Lord. He loved and He lived it to the grave. The very love He died for also resurrected Him to conquer all death, all darkness, all despair, and all destruction. He came to resurrect what we had destroyed. He invited us to join Him in crying out everywhere into the dark for anyone who would cry back. Through Him we would bring light into darkness, hope to despair, creation to destruction, and courage to death, after we ourselves had received life.

He was first up in the morning to see the sunrise and last to sleep at night so He could talk to his friends and his Father. He liked to see them sleeping and dream for them. He was first to pray, He would stand in the fray; He had no reverse. He would be still or go forward, pressing toward life. He loved His friends; never gave up on them, never wanted to leave them, but gave his life for them. He loved the needy. He loved his people. He even loved His enemies, and gave His life for them, too. He believed all things, walked through all things, and fought beyond all things to get to me and to you. He sat in grief, mourned our condition, called for us to awaken, reached to gather us in, dared us to reach back from within ourselves with a cry out. He walked with courage, dignity and humility, and He, in agony, begged His Father for help that both knew would not come until His heart's passion and vision were finished on the cross, and beyond. I bet they talked about that part a long time before Jesus came to us, because He was going to have to walk through hell alone for us.

Something in me moved. Jesus knew what life felt like, and He did not reject or discard those of us who failed, covered up, or even quit. Quite the opposite. "The Son of Man came to seek and save what was lost." (Luke 19:10) He called out into our wilderness of wandering and rigid self-righteousness for our hearts to turn toward our hope and cry out. He called into our defiance and resignation, our compromise and isolation. He refused our refusal. He came for us who had hidden truth, lost the way, and were missing our lives while living.

I did not just think about Him when I read the book. My heart wanted to be with Him. I wanted to get to Him. Something in me uncoiled and rose to see Him as true. It would be months and months before I would understand more of where I was going, but I didn't care. I got hope back in 1989 and it was in Him, so I followed the hope that would be fulfilled in Him.

In 1975, I walked down the concrete corridors to an exit into the dark with no ability to come back. Adrift from believing in love, care, family, friends, fathers, mothers, belonging, mattering, trusting, giving, staying, or attaching. But in 1989 I got hope back. Golla risked partnering with me to start the counseling center. I followed her lead, and I began to learn about Who my hope was in. I began to learn how to stand and stay with heart. In 1991, I met a therapist named Bruce who walked me to the bottom of myself by taking me all the way into my depths and helping me struggle to bring my insides outside. He walked me into the admission and surrender and acceptance of heart. I wrote my Dad letters; I told him the truth about my heart. I was filling up. I was also becoming a Dad to two young sons, and a man to a woman who feared to trust her heart with me. I had harmed most *wow* –

who I loved most, mainly by trying to make her love me (she already did) while denying that I needed anything at all (she would have to fail). Insane, sickness, and sin this is, and tragically real.

I had admitted that I was deeply and completely in need. Without knowing yet what God was doing with me, I saw that I was living in the Beatitudes. I was living in the greatest sermon ever spoken. Blessed are the poor in spirit— the bankrupt, needy, desperate, empty, lost, homeless, and hopeless—for theirs is the kingdom of heaven's life opening up.

I look back over the mercy of God as I write this story, and I thank Golla for her living God and Sonya for her faith that she clung to like a child, my Dad's recovery from darkness, and my mother for following him into the light. On and on I could list person after person who gave me their hands and heart, even when I was blind to see.

The admission of neediness, the reawakening to the impossibility of love without hurt, or becoming whole without help, or cared about by earning it began in a cry out to the One who could repair my heart. I entered the Beatitudes in 1989, having remembered feeling them before in childhood, and have been walking through them ever since one day at a time into a life that could not have happened without God doing it. I can hardly believe it still. I began to experience the poverty of the sinful woman, the grief of Peter, the meekness of David, and the living words as alive.

For most of us, God touches our lives not in a package or an event as much as in transitions, wooings, lurings, and retracing us over and over to bring us to Him and bring us to ourselves so we can see. Sometimes He brings us slowly, sometimes fast, but mostly slowly to see through the eyes of our hearts clearly. He longs for us to be who we are made to be so we can do what we were created to do. I am hungry for Him still while filled by Him. More than ever I was beginning to be hungry for others to know Him.

key
here ✶

Before - no real compulsion to bring others into deadness of legalism + numbness ...

> Blessed are those who hunger and thirst
> for righteousness, for they will be filled.

God says in Ephesians 2 that we, you and I, are His masterpiece, even His poem. We are being written line by line in the blood of life and spirit of love as far as we can read. God desires to complete the poem in full living, loving, and leading lines of regeneration and recreation. He says that we are made in the LORD Jesus Christ in the beginning to have full life and to be a part of the beauty of what is true, noble, right, pure, lovely, admirable, anything excellent or praiseworthy. We receive this life by receiving Him through grace into open hearts. By grace through faith, we step into a life most of us never knew we could have. I didn't.

Blessed are those who hunger and thirst for righteousness, for more of the One who has done so much already

so different from rigid religion, doing, ignoring passions & feelings for life, which makes us numb & dumb

(for more of what they have seen or heard from God); they will be filled with daily bread and more. I had become hungry and thirsty, eating much, surprised by what was happening, yet I was still distrustful, secretly waiting for my believing to be my foolishness. Even evidence of how far He had brought me did not yet remove or settle my fear. I needed so much more of Him.

I remember a character in the comic strips named Charlie Brown. He was someone who kept looking for life and in spite of plenty of experience to convince him to give up, he continued to look for good and purpose. Another character, Lucy, would always convince him to try to kick a football while she held it in the placekicking position on the ground. "Come on, Charlie Brown, I'm not going to move it this time, I promise." Just as he would take the last step to kick the ball, believing Lucy really did want relationship and goodness for them, she would move the ball. He would miss, do a flip in the air and land on his back staring at the empty sky. Lucy would snicker, walk off with the ball, leaving Charlie Brown alone. In so many ways, the truth was I remained a wolf underneath lizard skin and a little boy in my heart, scared to believe that such love could really be true. To this very day, nearly two decades later, I still wake up amazed at God. Not so much that the ball didn't move as much as He has never left. He came to stay. It's kind of like He can't leave. Leaving is not in His nature. We do the leaving.

Jesus said, "I have come that they (we) may have life, and have it to the full." (John 10:10) He said that in His will, in His hands, we become who we were created to become. When the fourth Beatitude comes, we have already seen more, found more, and have more. And He in His magnificence says there still exists more. He says to us that you will desire more than how you presently survive. You will hunger and thirst to have more of what you are finding in me. God says to us that we the redeemed can trust the following words:

> You are my masterpiece; you are my poetry, my poem, let me do for you what you will never do for yourself. Let me place you in right standing to know that you have been declared good enough, that you are looked at by me as true, noble, right, pure, lovely, admirable, excellent, and praiseworthy.

The fullness of the life we seek is found in righteousness, being made fit for Him, set upright, looked at and found good enough or justified. Jesus said because of me, you are found righteous, good enough, and your work is to believe in me: "The work of God is this: to believe in the one he has sent." (John 6:29) Just like Abraham believed God and that believing was credited to him as righteousness (Genesis 15:6), good enough for the holy God, so now believe in me and be filled with who I am and what I do. Jesus is our righteousness.

Jesus said about himself, "For the bread of God is he who comes down from heaven and gives life to the world." (John 6:33) Then, in the midst of others' distrust, he declares, "I am the bread of life. He who comes to me will never go hungry, and he who believes in me will never be thirsty.... All that the Father gives me will come to me, and whoever comes to me I will never drive away." (John 6:35, 37)

Blessed are those who hunger and thirst for more of Who has found them and they have found. He declares me good enough. He makes me into who I am made to be, to do what I am made to do. It is as if Jesus says to us, "I will make you good enough, place you in right standing, be with you, hear you, talk to you, direct you, be present with you every step of the way. You are hungry and thirsty. I am righteousness. You be human. I will be God. I will take you as far as you are willing to go and fill you with as much as you can hold."

"Come on," Jesus is saying, as ridiculous or trite as this may sound, "Come on, kick the ball, come." He doesn't move it.

I had missed much by just surviving. I wanted to live. He had life. I wanted Him and life. Gratitude is a funny thing. It requires a lot of sadness.   *wow — so true...*

CHAPTER
FIVE

BLESSED ARE THE MERCIFUL, FOR
THEY WILL BE SHOWN MERCY.

I did indeed get to help Golla start Bent Tree Counseling Center. She was able to borrow/rent temporary space from the person who supported the idea of a counseling center initially. He had been a big supporter of her recovery and an early caregiver when her journey of recovery first started. It began as a sliding scale Christian counseling place dedicated to meet people at their point of need, imposing nothing but exposing hearts to the possibility of life beyond survival.

Under her stewardship, we moved from borrowed space to 5,000 square feet of office space in one and a half years, and I became the clinical director with eight other therapists who had joined us. I grew, too, discovering along the way that in God's economy of surrender, nothing from our past does God waste.

When we give back over that which is actually His in the first place, surrender, He truly does what we cannot do for ourselves. He replenishes where there was scarcity, redeems what had become worth little, restores the abandoned places, reawakens that which was numbed, and recreates in the midst of destruction. He can even resurrect, make rise again, what is dead. Jesus said of Himself that He came to give good news to the poor, gather up shattered hearts, provide freedom for captives, release the imprisoned from darkness, make vengeance against death, comfort all who mourn, give beauty for ashes and oil of gladness instead of endless tears, and cover us in a garment of praise instead of a spirit of despair. Those He touches with His "re" longings will be called "oaks of righteousness, a planting of the LORD for the display of his splendor." (Isaiah 61:1-3) He grows us from roots of planting to a harvest of splendor. Our God is a "re" God.

The Bible I had once only read began to be alive with the heart of God, even the books that spoke of the edge of God now mattered. My construction background, my descent and hopelessness, my background and present, even my ugliness became others' hope. Some years later Golla would say about me, "God sought a man; then a man sought God; man of God." I remember hearing those words and wincing, for to know change is to remember also the depth of change needed. Both grateful and humbled at once. I worked so hard to be big, to become somebody I could not be, instead of who I am. I was never big; God has simply decided that you and I are "big deals," worth the trouble. God delights in trouble. God delights in his own creation. He sent His Son to show us we are big deals and to bring us back to life. The more we give Him the truth of our hearts, the more room there is in us for Him to live, love and lead. The more He does, the more we wind up living fully, loving deeply, and leading well—in that order.

Over a period of six years, in this crucible of getting to be alive in others' lives and in my own life, with God, I not only grew, but also began to formulate from within about paying forward. Recreated people create, replenished people have plenty to speak and give, drawing from the well that never runs dry of God's supply of Himself, others, and of their own heart's dreams.

Clumsily, reforming, embattled and grateful, I moved forward, working and sometimes resting in mercy, in being a man with Sonya, a dad to two young sons, and one who was doing what he was made to do.

I began to experience the ancient of all truths as true: bidden or unbidden, God is present. We experience the presence of Him when we ourselves finally come to the place of powerlessness and face that we cannot fix ourselves, or really fix anything. We admit powerlessness and need. It equals neediness. He does it. We, if we receive Him, then get to participate and share in what He is doing. We are grateful to have received so much mercy. We want to participate in what God is doing. We who have been rescued from where we were, and from where we were headed, begin to see ourselves in everyone and we become compelled to participate in the act of gratitude.

I remember a time after we moved into the first house we built in Flower Mound, Texas, Sonya came home one afternoon and found me planting flowers in a large flower bed that I had made for her. She had come through the house, walked out under the wisteria-covered arbor into the backyard, seeing me before I saw her. Apparently she watched me planting the flowers and patting the dirt for a minute or two before she said something. I turned, stood up, smiling and stepping toward her as she walked toward me. She said later that she loved me so then and knew how much I loved her. I had stepped into her heart's love of flowers and beauty without doing it for her approval. No *quid pro quo*. I had stepped into the interest of her interests. When we love someone we join him or her in the joy of his or her interests, not the interest itself necessarily. We need to do so because God has knitted them together in this way, and love expands in an exponential way by joining with who they are.

She caught me on my knees loving her without her around. That spiritual moment surprised her, to see prayers answered in the backyard of a subdivision like others on an otherwise ordinary day.

When God is not refused by someone—that is that—He does not stop. He cares and He cannot stop, and He desires for us to see and grow and not stop, too. But He does it. That is what His mercy to us is all about. He does what we can't do on our own. He does it all the time. He saves us, heals us,

I have been made to see life thru God's mercies — that are new every morning — wow

grows us, sculpts us into this masterpiece we were created by Him to become. We cannot create ourselves. He is the sculptor who knocks and chips away at the stone until we are revealed. And we, tragically, can refuse the brokenness to receive the mercy He offers us in grace. His mercies are new everyday, and we are made to see life through them.

Three years after starting Bent Tree, Golla asked our new executive administrator and myself to attend a leadership conference at a mega church near Chicago called Willow Creek. I attended the conference, not doubting God as much as doubtful about true fellowship occurring in a mega anything. And I was still cautious about believing in God's goodness, as in, when would He be Lucy to my Charlie Brown? However, I was terribly willing to follow Jesus' trail—if not fully his lead. I still, sadly, kept some distance until the day I ran heart long into a dead end of pride and arrogance at this church amidst a fellowship of believers. I slammed into what mercy grants us; God clearly let me know that His grace is sufficient and my pride or assistance is altogether unnecessary.

The experience from the conference that has stayed with me occurred in the auditorium during a time of worship. God retraced me again to let me have more of Him and more awareness of myself. From inside the sanctuary I could see out massive windows, into an expanse of a lake, geese, sky, trees and grass. Someone led a song of worship. I looked out the windows, glad to have been a part of the conference, to get to see a larger picture of the church beyond my doubt and distrust. We would fly back to Texas the next morning. The view of life outside was beautiful and the music of praise inside was rich. I thought this time of worship was a well-done conclusion to a good conference.

Then I began to have a daydream while I was singing. In the daydream I saw myself forgiven, not of the big, but of all the little things that make up the big. I saw manipulation, deceit, greed, control, lying, distrust, and anticipation unbuckle from around my waist, like a heavy tool belt dropping to the ground.

I stopped singing. And then I began to see World War I. I sat in a trench shaking inside, squatted with my back pressed against the hard clay trench wall. Many of us were placed in this ditch in a long line. Above the trench the ground was fortified by barbed wire and wooden barriers—old warfare preparation. I saw no faces, but I could feel my own face. The sounds of war exploded above me and away from my back in the distance, like a thousand hooves galloping toward us.

The landscape of war above me was filled with misty smoke and the sounds of fear and power. The earth was scarred and burned. Leafless trunks of trees charcoaled into lifelessness were all around. The bare ground was a mixture of soot and hard, rutted metal, making running across it quickly impossible. There was no life on it, and I had been assigned to attack across it.

We had been given orders to move in the direction of the roar of dying. They had already yelled, "Move, move, attack!" And I was sitting in that trench with my back against the wall, saying, "Go, go, go, charge the enemy," to myself. And I knew that as soon as I moved, I was, barring a miracle, certainly going to die. I was prepared to go. It was time to go. But I was so scared that I couldn't move.

I could hear amidst all the noise, and my internal words, my own breathing, and then another explosion and a dirt clod fall beside my head and scatter at my feet. My wool uniform was heavy with sweat, my rifle pointing straight up in the air between my knees, and the butt of my gun that stabbed into the ground weighed a thousand pounds. I hated my fear. I was desperate to stay put, not move, not get killed but knew I would have to go. My mind pounded, "Go, go, go," but my body wouldn't release my heart's fear.

I heard someone's voice beside me. A fellow soldier, dressed like me, somehow seemed like a friend I knew or had known. In my peripheral glance, not turning my own head, I saw a young experienced face—set eyes, heart of contained passion, straight fire, a war-wizened face. His uniform had no special marks on it. I could tell that he was looking at me by his voice, but I could not turn my head to see. He said, "I'll go for you." It registered to me as a kind gesture, and at the same time, I took it as exposing me with insult. Amidst all the noise, all the anonymity of me, I realized that he had possession of himself enough to see me. What he saw was my terror and neediness, despair without rescue, and my willingness. I was just so scared. I couldn't yet muster the pride to move. He knew that I knew death had come, and yet my paralysis in that war trench on that day was, perverse as it sounds, a hope, a squeaky, baby bird-mouthed sound of hope. Hope that my death wouldn't be too painful; hope that at least I could do it with dignity by facing it. And even a hope that I could live, though I knew I wouldn't. Surely, I had that much faith.

I shook out words in my pride, somehow seeking understanding. I said, "No, I'm going," meaning I really do plan to go any second now but I'm terrified. like someone flailing while they are free falling from a cliff, desperately seeking a reversal of fortune.

I was angry at his insulting offer and arrogance that made us unequal. He looked at me with strength and care, eyes searching, clear and focused. He said, "I'm going for you." But I continued to resist, saying, "No," without turning my head, just as he moved quickly, and climbed from the trench onto the ground of hell on earth. I reached instinctively at what I thought was his judgment of me as a coward. My hand landed on the back of his heel. I didn't need his help, or his arrogant bravery to help me. His boot heel slipped through my futile grab to pull him back down. Without thinking I leapt toward him with furious desperation trying to stop him from getting killed and making my own upcoming death worse. It was the only courage I had and so I ran with it, not caring for myself but for the sudden awakening of fear again. I was running madly across the battlefield chasing someone; I didn't know his name, but I remembered his voice. I needed to catch up with him.

I ran to stop him in order to save him. But I couldn't find him anywhere. Gone. I knew he was headed into the teeth of the fire, so that is where I ran. In patchy, suffocating smoke, my own breath echoing in my head; only two sounds I heard, war and breathing. Broken trees, bare ground, darkness, destruction, despair, death. I'm alone in war, running to nowhere. I was lost and running hard.

Then it was all gone. I stopped running. I stood within a circle of quiet. Soaking wet in a smothering wool uniform, I dropped to the bare, burned, salty ground when I finally find him and see that he is dying. They got him. He hung from a cross, strung out and crushed, dying, stripped and bloody. Oh, God, no!

He gasped for air. I screamed at him in hate-filled anguish of desperation to get down; let me up there. "Please...please, let me get up there. Don't; please, don't do this to me. I can't handle it. I just can't do it anymore."

He looked at me, seeing me with eyes still tragically alive in a savaged body. He said, "You cannot do it." I fell on the ground, broken, humiliated, and contemptuous of my own powerlessness and pride and broken by my humiliating gratefulness. I couldn't save myself, make myself or fix myself, my life or anyone else's. He did it. He does it.

He lives. He loves. He leads. By the right of conquering He does so. Even more, by the Presence of love, He does so. His love overtook, and conquered, and redeemed us from darkness, destruction, despair, and death. We still refuse our fulfillment. We are sick with refusal.

The confusion of love and hate ripped through me. His love was doing what I couldn't. Don't do this. Oh, Jesus, please don't. Oh, Jesus, thank you. I'm sorry, thank you. Please don't go. Please stay. Oh, don't die. Oh, don't, not for me. Does life have to be this way?

There I lay on iron ground, broken, rescued, desperate, grateful, alive and on a battlefield in a war without end in sight. His courage was for me. His life was for me. His love to keep on was for me. I saw all these truths and quietly cried in amazement and gratitude.

And I loved Him back even more than before. Grace rescued me from my own ego. I had been broken to pieces, smashed into Him and not crushed. So I tell you, wherever He goes, I want to be there—with the Hero.

I saw the big sins, that are just unavoidable, the ones I could confront myself about. But He rescued me from a deeper death.

Instead of the armor of a warrior, I wore the tool belt of a survivor—which made me crafty. The belt was loaded with tools to succeed—tools of deceit, demand, manipulation, defiance, niceness, judgment, assumptions, compromise, presumptions, grandiosity, resignation, apathy, a lack of conscience, approval-seeking, cowardice, denial, justification, and envy, all feeding off of a heart created in His image for life, not for survival.

His grace went after everything, still does, and those "little" flaws and ego-willed defenses will continue to birth harm to others and my very being. The "bigger" sins on my outer world arose from the seeds of secrecy around my own heart; I built them using all the tools of survival that were refusing His redemption, rescue, and recreation.

Since then, and even now, when I hear someone speak of receiving grace, I ask, "Was it painful?" If they tell me, "No," I wonder what would make me so different. "Was I that bad and that desperate?" I ask myself. "I guess so," I conclude and thank God for His rescuing me—for continuing to retrace me, bringing me to Him and His intentions as I surrender more and more to having Him and having my life. For me, being touched by grace through His mercy was the most terrific pain. Being loved "in spite of...", and being rescued in the midst of desperate exposure and powerlessness even now helps me remember. I remember the tragedy of life, the glory of Him, and I wince in gratitude still. What He paid for, what I could not do, and what He paid in spite of what I had done, cost Him everything. He paid for my freedom, a ransom for the one who was captured; I took it.

He says to me and you that our rescue and recreation is worth everything. You and I are worth all of Jesus' life, death, and rising again. I had once thought I was worth very little, ultimately, but for what I could scrape together. He says that nothing I could "scrape" together, or build, or do, or amass, can make me worthy or earn what I need. He does it. He decided that I am worth His movements, created in His image, and He wants me back so He can finish what He started.

He has passion for me, and compassion toward me. He also knew what being human is like, remembering that we are dust, unable to do what only He can do. He is even able to remove our transgressions from us, as far as the east is from the west. (Psalm 103:12) He gave me mercy, passionate compassion, and gave me grace, a divine acceptance. He let me see how great and compassionate, good and abounding in love He is.

Merciful liberation is from Him. I do not earn it, but I can make Him small again by forgetting or removing myself from the truth of my own heart's experience. That day, that moment, when I saw Jesus and heard Him on the cross was not an event, but an opportunity, not one thing to cling to but something to remember and walk on into from where I had already come. Process.

But how do I remember without having to make lists, and labor not to forget, and try hard, push for it, or make it happen? How do I stay with the truth of my heart without returning to the way I always did everything? How do I remain in the light, in hope, in creation, and in courage while darkness, destruction, despair, and death surround me? How do I remember God and stay with God in this tragic life, believing and walking in His faithfulness? How do I live the liberty I could not earn?

The answer was so simple even then it took a long time to gain footing on the path of not returning and not forgetting. Surrender daily.

I surrender every single morning that I walk this earth who I am to Whose I am. Surrender literally means to render or give back over. It implies that I am returning something (someone) I took, and I was left free to steal (him) away if I so willed it. Surrender is not defeat. I surrender to the truth that God made me to be a God-sized project rather than a man-sized project. I need all His Presence and movements to let the desires He put in my heart to come true and grieve into acceptance when they do not come true. Either way, God is present and available.

So every day, every morning before the day begins, I give myself to Him who can do with me what I never would have been able to do with me. He can build me, convert me, trace me, mold me, and fill me from the inside out. Every morning I agree with Him that I am in need and I am in need of who He is. I thank Him for what He has done already, remembering my life before and now. I thank Him for giving me the highest position a human being can have, servant-emissary to the King of Kings. I tell Him that I need Him. To be in agreement with God means to confess. In surrender, then, I confess my need, and then I give my heart over to Him, to be blessed with more of who He is and what He has for me.

Again, surrender is not defeat and weakness. No. Surrender in need of heart is the doorway into living our liberation, remembering who we were made to be, and staying in the quest of living His mercy.

Our God in our surrender to His compassion speaks to us, guiding us in the paths of His ways through His Word, prayer, circumstances, other people, and illumination (letting us see and imagine more of Him with us.) In our surrender, you and I see Him by knowing Him and hear by listening for Him. And He brings more, including an attitude of recognizing ourselves in others. Those who have received mercy, give mercy. Those who give mercy, passionate compassion, receive even more mercy in the midst of increasing dependence upon God. There still exists a world of darkness, destruction, despair, and death that awaits our lantern—bringing our artistry, our hoping and our courage to others. Those who have taken God's passionate compassion will receive even more a heart of love and desire to conquer all that is tragic. The merciful do not judge for they were not judged. Instead, they attend to living, and the merciful are available to those who have forgotten who they are and need light in the dark, creation in destruction, hope in despair, and courage in death. The merciful give what they have received. And God gives them more of who He is and what He does through others and Himself. Blessed are the merciful for they will be shown mercy.

I referred earlier to the first question God ever asked: "Where are you?" (Genesis 3:9) The question was filled with mercy and it was God's first movement toward mankind's redemption. Tell me where you are, speak the truth of your heart, so I can meet you in your need. Feel your feelings, tell the truth, and give it to God. This question is not asked so much for God to measure us, as much as for God to restore us. He asks this question over and over until our last moment of breath with a much greater love than a loving mother or father who reaches to care for a child, so they

Stop denying &
not thinking about
what hurts — then
give it to God... so we
dont get stuck in despair

can walk the child to strength. God desires for us the end of our ego sufficiency, the vows of will power, and pride in our possession, so we can become fully who He made us to be. That question is the question I answer every morning from the inside out to the One who desires intimacy with me.

The Place of your Presence

"Where are you?" presents the moment of actual mercy awaiting a heart to receive liberation. The presence of God awaits answer to the question that calls to our inside life. His presence is near. He pursues but does not intrude. We are not alone, and yet because He does not go where He is not invited, we are presented with a personal crisis. We can risk exposure and have need of more than I myself can make, or we can maintain contempt against our own needs of heart and miss God and His creativity. Crisis means danger, yes. But crisis also means opportunity. We often run from the opportunity of love in fear, contempt and judgment of such mercy because it exposes us as human in need of God, as longing and thus unable to complete ourselves. We must become sick of running away and willing to run toward. Then, we find that "Where are you?" is God in search of who He loves.

"Where are you?" is not an accusation,
but an opportunity;
not about perfection, but about confession;
not a proving time, but a neediness invitation;
not letting God discover, but about seeing
our own character;

not about achievement, but about redemption;

not will sufficiency, but God-made ability;

not about strength, but about trust;

not about power, but about presence;

not about should do, but about get to;

not about seeking explanation, but about recreation;

not about subordination, but about submission;

not about determination, but about passion for us.

I have the privilege of surrendering to Him and His character every day.

Genesis 4 records a story of the tragedy of rejecting the question "Where are you?" and the defeat of lives if we do not find surrender. God offered Cain this same question, so He could have him see who he was made to be so he could do what he was made to do. God told Cain that he could have what his heart hungers and thirsts for, but just not his way. I am God; you are humankind. Let go of being God. Face your need to be fully human, fully in relationship with you, others and me. God pursued Cain; Cain refused God's love, never surrendering into a relationship with the Creator of life. God wished to "delight over (him) with singing and quiet (him) with his love." (Zephaniah 3:17), but Cain refused.

Here is how the story goes. Cain and Abel were brothers, the sons of Adam and Eve, who had hidden their hearts from the LORD God, breaking relationship with God by figuring instead of feeling, silencing the heart over crying out for Presence.

"Now Abel kept flocks and Cain worked the soil. In the course of time," (Genesis 4:2-3) the story goes, "Cain brought some of the fruits of the soil as a recognition to the LORD." (vs. 3) Abel brought an offering also, "fat portions from some of the firstborn of his flock." (vs. 4) What Abel gave was the richest, best or finest of that which came first, expressing not only a recognition of Creator, but a gratitude and sense of trust or well-being in a tragic life of toil. Abel's heart was known to God and he recognized the LORD as God with us.

Cain, however, exposed a closed disposition of heart, one secreted away in a place of distrust and resentment, and thus away from the touch of God.

I fear that Cain gave God an orphan's present. Years ago when I worked construction, I worked with a fellow named Stan who later became an architect. Stan had grown up in an orphanage, never chosen or pursued by parents. He had had his heart broken deeply. Yet as a man he became someone who taught me a great deal about a loving God. Stan had a relationship with God, one of gratitude, like one who had been lost in the dark and Someone came and found him. He had a heart of knowing the difference between despair and hope. He shared with me one time about Christmas at the orphanage, how often what the children received were old, used, or even broken toys. They were the gifts from the family members of sponsoring churches. Stan told me this story without bitterness, yet clearly with a sad and angry recognition of all that the story means about us human beings. Cain gave to God like those people "gave" to Stan.

After Cain gave God the offering, what he had earned by the bend of his back and the sweat of his brow, God found no connection to Cain's heart. God comes to Cain and offers the first of many opportunities. It is like God said to Cain, "Where are you, Cain? Speak the truth of your heart so that I might save you, be with you and you know me." God sought his heart. "Why are you angry? Why is your face downcast? If you do what is right, will you not be accepted? But if you do not do what is right, sin is crouching at the door, but you must master it." (Genesis 4:6-7)

If "Where are you?" is mercy that offers favor, then God showed Cain favor or the longing He has for us to have life. "Tell me, Cain, about your bitterness, your hurt, your resentment, your distrust, even your hatred so I can rescue you. I made you free to be in relationship or to refuse it. Sin craves to get you."

Then God tells Cain that he "must master" (vs. 7) sin. The statement presents a paradox. No one can master sin for everyone needs the LORD to do for them what they cannot do. God offered Cain the impossible to offer him opportunity to admit that he could not do it, so God could. God is God; we are human.

As stated earlier, Jesus said to a very good man who sought to master sin in Matthew 19 that it is easier for a camel to go through the eye of a needle than for a rich man (or a man of personal sufficiency) to go to heaven.

The disciples said to him in dismay, then who can ꞏbe saved? "Jesus looked at them and said, 'With man this is impossible, but with God all things are possible.'" (Matthew 19:26) Jesus said what mankind does not have dynamite to do (impossible or *exdunamai*, in the Greek) God has dynamite to do (possible or *dunamai*). God does the saving and the salving (healing), but we have to admit the needing. needing. Cain rejected both initial offerings, deciding like so many of us to take things into his own hands—refusing to answer the question and refusing healing.

He hated, resented, projected, and externalized, and then his refusal turns into premeditated action. Cain relieved his hatred of his condition by getting twisted justice against one who depended on God. He killed his brother to avoid his own admission of neediness.

God came to Cain again and asked, "Where is your brother, Abel?" (Genesis 4:9) Come to me, Cain, God calls. "Come unto me, all who labor and are heavy laden and I will give you rest. Take my yoke upon you and learn from me, for I am gentle and humble in heart and you will find rest for your souls. For my yoke is easy and my burden is light," (Matthew 11:28-29) Jesus said. He has spoken these words from the beginning. Was He not offering Himself to Cain, too?

Cain refuses again quickly and furiously, "I don't know. Am I my brother's keeper?" (Genesis 4:9) He lies about himself, his own heart, and to God, and then exposes his contempt for all of life's dependencies, especially the need of God. "Am I my brother's keeper" has a sneer and disgust-filled undertone to it. *Today's culture mentality*

"Am I my brother's keeper?" Jesus tells the story of the Good Samaritan to answer this question, recorded in Luke 10:30-37. A band of thieves had jumped one man, stripped him of his clothes, beaten him, and left him to die. He was naked, rendered a vagrant, and poor in spirit. A priest saw him and passed by. A Levite saw him and passed by on the other side. But a Samaritan, one who by birth in that country would have known rejection, heartache, nakedness, and poverty of spirit somewhere in his life, had found God's merciful healing along his journey of life. For this Samaritan "as he travelled, came to where the man was;" and when he saw him, he had passionate compassion (mercy) on him. He went to him and "bandaged his wounds, pouring oil and wine. Then he put the man on his donkey, took him to an inn and took care of him. The next day he took out two silver coins and gave them to the innkeeper. 'Look after him,' he said, 'and when I return, I will reimburse you for any extra expense you may have.'" (vv. 34-35)

As a Samaritan, he certainly knew rejection and heartache, and probably bitterness and cynicism. A Samaritan in the hierarchical world of that culture was considered cursed, unclean, and was purposefully avoided by the "right" people. He easily could have seen himself as needing to give nothing for no one had given to him. Instead, somewhere in his life, he had fallen in his brokenness through the door of the first Beatitude, admitted neediness,

grieved his losses, received healing, hungered and thirsted
for more of who God was making him, and then desired to
give it away. Blessed are the merciful, for they will be shown
mercy. Our God desires to lead us to His mercy so that we
can even be shown more and more of who He is and what
He does. Our God desires for us to turn and offer what we
have received after we have received. The Samaritan did
just that. God does not offer Cain or the Samaritan or me
what we earned. He pursues us with a gift of mercy. He
gives the opposite of what we have earned.

God offers Cain another crisis, another opportunity
to answer the question so healing and life can be restored
to him. God says to Cain, "Now you are under a curse and
driven from the ground...when you work the ground, it
will no longer yield its crops for you. You will be a restless
wanderer on the earth." (Genesis 4:11-12) This curse is not
condemnation, and being driven from the land is not death.
God offers to let Cain have the future that isolation will
bring, so he sends him to the desert, so to speak. The desert
in spiritual writings is the place of discovering God, a place
where a man cries out in dependence, ending one's own
sufficiency—or the man dies. He can admit humanity or he
can play God.

This curse is by no means condemnation or death, for
when Cain complains that "the punishment is more than
I can bear...and whoever finds me will kill me," (vs. 13-14)
God says to him that He would place a seal of protection on
Cain that no physical harm would come to him. He protected

him from death so that condemnation would not happen. He sought Cain even as Cain rejected Him; but Cain took God's mercy and walked away from His presence. Instead of crying out, Cain headed straight for the land of Nod and began to build a city—a fortified encampment extending from his calloused heart, all to keep him from needing, asking, or answering God's mercy. No more conversations; The distractions and productions of the city he built could block him from even hearing the whispers of the night coming from inside that said, "There is more, Cain. Where are you, Cain?" A twenty-four hour a day distraction of the city, like an addicted culture, deafens us and blinds us to God's presence near us.

In Matthew 22:1-5, Jesus said the kingdom of heaven is like a king who prepared a marvelous wedding banquet to celebrate the life of his son. The king imagined, designed, and created. When it was prepared, the king smiled because of how joyous he felt inside to look upon all that was very good. The streamers were streaming, the candles were burning, the banquet was warming, the seats were available, so he sent his servants to all those he had invited to come, for everything was ready.

But they refused.

Did God long to have Cain? Yes.

Did God condemn Cain? No.

We can refuse God's mercy, reject Gods longing for us, snuff out the answer to the moment-to-moment question, and wind up missing our lives.

———

Cain rejected the first Beatitude of neediness and missed the inheritance of the kingdom of heaven. He refused what was very, very good. Then he missed the second Beatitude, the need to grieve this tragic life, which would bless him with the wings of securing Comfort and certain support. Cain lost the third Beatitude, the opportunity to serve and passionately participate in something greater than himself, leaving a legacy of creation on earth. He rejected the truth that we are created to hunger and thirst for more, even more than what we have already received from the Righteous One, and so he would never be filled. Cain then turned his face away from that which makes life worth living: passionate compassion, the gratitude of heart to remember who we are and Whose we are—which allows us to give freely and love deeply. He put up his fist against the grace of mercy. Unfortunately, even Cain's hope became despair, his fires darkened, and his forging destruction led to his own heart death.

Blessed are the merciful, for they will be shown mercy.

Are we not all sons and daughters of Cain in need of transformation into emissaries of a King? Those who have received the blessings of the first five Beatitudes can do no less than have the eyes of their hearts focused upon the One who gives life and wish to give life to their own relatives.

When I was young I knew that God was like cool green fescue and could paint with colors like blue and yellow. He loved the sounds of meadowlarks in spring and fall, rolling thunder, rain and laughter. He knew the sounds of birds' wings that fly over in flocks and the spice of a persimmon. He liked sparrows and pumpkins, our feelings and the sun, baseball and His son. He was crazy about His son; they talked all of the time. God sent Him to tell us all about these things He liked, how much He liked us, and what He is like, and we killed Him for it. I did not understand that part when I was young. I do now. I'm still sad about it, but I am also very, very grateful because I once was blind, but now I see. I once was lost, even to my own memory of Him, and now I am found. Amazing grace. Life is created by God and is very good; life is also tragic. And God is faithful. We find His faithfulness in our surrender. His faithfulness also awakens us to desire others to be freed from the prison of isolation we once survived.

Living the liberation, remembering and staying free, begins every day with surrender, joining the Will of God, who is the Maker of Life. He gives us more and more, shows us more and more, for our God is the God of abundance.

Live fully, Love deeply, Lead well.

The merciful live fully because they have been given life; they love deeply because they have been loved completely; they lead well because they listen for, look for, and follow His leading.

———

Passion, Intimacy, and Integrity.

The merciful have a passion, a willingness to be in pain for something greater than aversion to pain because He came to do for us, which allows us to see. His compassion becomes our passion. The merciful live in intimacy or "into-me-see" with their own hearts, others, and God because relationship brings fulfillment. They are known and know. The merciful move in integrity, from the front door of one's self, throughout the interior of one's self, and to the back of one's self. The substance of integrity speaks trustworthiness because God has given us ourselves, to become ourselves, to have the joy of giving ourselves away, and to be a part of creation.

Feel feelings, Tell truth, Give it to God.

All of this occurs through the simplest child process of life. We experience what we feel within us (please see *The Voice of the Heart*), we tell the truth about our hearts, and we give this inner truth to the processes of God. The story of our life then unfolds. A whole reformation of a person occurs. A person cries out. God "shows up." God raises them up. That person steps out, bringing light into darkness, hope into despair, creation into destruction, and courage into death.

What does it mean to be shown mercy? Psalm 118 begins with the following verse: "Give thanks to the LORD, for he is good; his mercy endures forever." (Psalm 118:1) His mercy, care and love for us opens us up to experience His goodness. The list below defines goodness. It is long and has more to it than can practically be written about in this book, but the list reflects what it means to be shown mercy. His mercy shows us His goodness. We see, experience, struggle with, and live in the goodness He has given us.

GOOD

beautiful	fruitful
excellent	economical
lovely	beneficial
convenient	precious
aesthetic	favor
pleasant	gracious
delightful	kind
sound	ready
righteous	sweet
joyful	wealth
virtue	welfare
practical	pleasure
cheerful	best
sensual	well
correct	true

In the book of Micah, the prophet speaks of God's desire when he writes, "He has showed you, O man, what is good. And what does the LORD require of you? To act justly, and to love mercy, and to walk humbly with your God." (Micah 6:8) The merciful get to live the mercy they have received and are shown even more. The merciful live the good life.

Please read Chip Dodd's *The Voice of the Heart: A Call to Full Living* for a fuller knowledge and deeper understanding of feelings, their purpose, and gifts.

CHAPTER
SIX

BLESSED ARE THE PURE IN HEART
FOR THEY WILL SEE GOD.

Early in Jesus' longed-for mission, He stood up in the synagogue in His hometown of Nazareth to read from the scroll of holy words. The scroll of the prophet Isaiah was handed to him (Luke 4:16-17). Jesus unrolled it, finding the place where the following words are written from Isaiah 61 that declare what He came to do:

The Spirit of the Sovereign LORD is on me, because the LORD has anointed me to preach good news to the poor. He has sent me to bind up the broken-hearted, to proclaim liberty for the captives and release from darkness for the prisoners, to proclaim the year of the LORD's favor and the day of vengeance of our God. To comfort all who mourn, and provide for those who grieve in Zion

---

to bestow on them a crown of beauty instead of
ashes, the oil of gladness instead of mourning, and a
garment of praise instead of a spirit of despair. They
will be called oaks of righteousness, a planting of the
LORD for the display of His splendor. (Isaiah 61: 1-3)

We are born into life crowned with neediness and
honored with dependency. We are also deemed to have great
inherent worth, certainly worth Him coming to do for us
what we could not do for ourselves. We were born just like
He made us. And He desires for us to remain with Him so we
become vessels that pour out springs of living water, instead
of beautifully painted vessels with no life within us.

Jesus tells those who have forgotten, those who have
refused, or those who have existed by pretending that "unless
you change and become like little children, you will never
enter the kingdom of heaven." (Matthew 18:3) Jesus says in a
sentence what the Scriptures testify to over and over again. By
admission of our neediness and surrender of our dependency
to Him, He does for us what we cannot do for ourselves. He
does what He said He came to do as quoted from Isaiah 61:1-3.

God grows us into "oaks of righteousness, a planting of
the LORD for the display of His splendor." The tree of our
lives comes from the roots that depend upon and need the
presence and provision of the Creator to grow the fruit of
life and its fulfillment. The roots reach deeply into God and
the limbs grow strong—displaying the splendor of God in
our lives.

Jesus came to set us free and then bless us even more by
our return to how we are made. He can set us free from our
egos—the shell around the true self that focuses upon the
approval of people, appearance, and "face". He can set us free
from reality to let us believe in the truth, free from grasping for
power so we can live truly present in life, and He can liberate
us from sufficiency in our methods to dependence upon His
great purposes.

He said, though, that no matter how much He calls,
many people will refuse because of the rejection of their own
hearts—hearts created in neediness and dependency to be
rooted in Him. Jesus says that in us is fulfilled the prophecy
of Isaiah (6:9-10).

> You will be ever hearing, but never understanding;
> you will be ever seeing, but never perceiving. For
> this peoples' heart has become calloused; they
> hardly hear with their ears and they have closed
> their eyes. Otherwise they might see with their
> eyes, hear with their ears understand with their hearts
> (italics mine) and turn, and I would heal them.
> (Matthew 3:14-15)

There it is, the clear line of demarcation between hearts
that will "see" and "hear" their need and dependency, admit
to the truth of life, and surrender their insides for healing and
growth into life, and those who will not. The healing is from
the inside—the roots—and then moves to the outside—the

fruit. We must recognize and give our feelings, needs, desires, longings, and hope—the roots of our beings—back to Him.

God pursues us to have us. He desires for us to give up on our vow of protection—because it does not work anymore. That which perhaps once suited us and justified our right to the "calloused" heart is now destroying all we are made to be and have. The protection of my heart from pain developed into egotism that suffocates the heart of neediness; my focus on control or power took the place of being truly present, even aware of myself and therefore, anyone else. My focus on being realistic blinded me from seeing the truth of God doing the impossible. And most tragic, my life of independence strangled every blessing, every gift, every touch of God that allows us great gratitude and awe, the outcome of dependence upon His creativity. My power kept me from being amazed. His presence allowed me to see.

The contrast creates two lives. The line between the two places is a battle line, whether we like it or not. The line is drawn between those who walk in the receptive heart, almost always made in brokenness and loss, and those who carry the heart of refusal, almost always calloused by a vow of protection against ever allowing neediness or dependence to occur again. God's favor moves to seek the needy and His vengeance is against the darkness that blinds us, the destruction that shatters our lives, the despair that renders us captive to hopelessness, and the death that makes us stifle the courage of our own cry out for grace to come upon us like new blood into dry bones. When we declare

When I declare my independence from God (arrogance—I know better than God how to run my life) I cut myself off from God's mercy & grace...

independence, we declare independence from mercy that brings us grace—the bounty of God. We destroy ourselves and miss life, ironically, through the very machinations that we think will give us life.

I want to offer a small, tragic story that speaks to the potential of a great life missed. I skip years ahead with this small story, but it speaks of big things.

Sonya and I and our two teenage sons were at Disney World one December not too long ago. Sonya and I waited for a ferry one morning to take us back to our resort from a time of looking around and having coffee. The boys were still sound asleep. The blue sky surrounded us. The sun shone remarkably bright on the water in the morning. A family came down to the docking area, clearly Southern like us. The accent tends to be a giveaway. A set of grandparents, parents, and an excited ten-year-old waited for the ferry, too. They asked directions about the boat's destination because they had reservations for breakfast where the young boy was going to eat with some Disney characters. The mom and son were excited. The dad laughed nearby the boy as he sat down on a bench. The grandmother smiled pleasantly at their surroundings, and giggled about something the young boy said. She rubbed the top of his head as he stepped toward the bench where his dad sat. The grandfather, neatly dressed in a pressed, plaid shirt, tucked in, stood erect, waiting. He appeared removed. I looked at him, kind of nodded my head slightly in greeting. I had already talked to the mother and father a bit about directions. He glanced at me with nothing on his face but straight lips. Sonya had told them where the restaurant was located, assuring them they had plenty of time to get there. The grandson grabbed the grandfather's hand for a moment before sort of dancing toward the water. The grandmother said tentatively something toward the grandfather. He quipped about "rather be on my bass boat fishing." The mother kind of smiled before turning away.

The grandson stopped dancing and stood near the bench by his dad, who said something about how he would rather be bass fishing, too, no longer paying attention to the son. The grandmother's face never shifted from her pleasant expression. But I watched their delight creep inward, if not stop, in the refusal of the grandfather to extend his heart into his own or anyone else's delight. He said that he would rather be somewhere else. Of course, his desire is okay. But, I tell you, the face, the tone, the words, the eyes, the movements of the people around him spoke poverty. He was missing his life with them. I realize there are a myriad of other scenarios that could be possible. But lest you believe that the darkness of refusal is some far off occurrence in another nation, see if it is not in our own homes, and especially in our own hearts. When I heard the grandfather and saw the others' reactions, their shuffling and shifting behaviors, I thought of times I shut down others who love me by refusing to care.

How often have I blocked my own blessings because of my need for independence—independence from risk of heart, from sensitivity, care, need, love, tenderness, interest, concern, loss, from courage, trust, need, or from simply

130

being bothered. I have so often been that man. How many champions never are discovered because they never risk enough heart to show up in the arena of life? How many men's families never receive the fullness of God because of their dammed hearts that block the flow of God's presence into the hearts in their domain? How often do we harden the soil of our hearts so we can't receive God's seeds of life? How often do we keep the roots of our true selves from God's soil; we stop our inner selves from being touched by God and grown by God.

The pure in heart do not refuse the arena of life. They surrendered their hearts sometime ago and now live rooted in God. They grow up into life. Pure speaks to being transformed away from where we were. Pure of heart becomes unadulterated by ego (easing God out) and self-will (control). Not only does it mean clear, sincere, or transparent, pure speaks to our character, the character of integrity. Am I who I say I am? Am I speaking truth of heart? Am I truthful with my agenda? Do I admit my humanity? Do I want good for others? Do I seek forgiveness? Do I offer forgiveness? Do I live in confession and courage? Do I love? Is my will placed before the presence of God's will? Am I truthful in God's presence or do I stay distant?

Integrity expresses our purity and what we are being transformed into. Integrity means to be integrated—no longer separated. From the exterior of ourselves, through the middle, to the back side of ourselves, the substance is of the same material. No little pockets of secrecy or pride pull us away from life or attempt to control it. Integrated (always integrating) people are aware of what is occurring in their hearts. They tell the truth about what occurs within them; they give their heart's truth to God, and to others whose hearts are known; and they create on the earth with passion. The life of the good has taken the place of survival for safety.

The pure in heart do not count sins as much as they face themselves, open up to God so they can continue to see who they are made to be and do what they are made to do. They listen for God's movements in trust; they follow God's footprints in faith; they even will experience God's silence as love, even when they cry out with questions. The pure in heart believe. They remember what God has already done, and are certain that He will continue to move, and they look for what He is doing. The pure in heart also see God, as in receive Him, feel Him, know Him. They love God and know full well that God loved them first.

The willingness to be truthful about the interior of one's own heart and to have confidence in God's trustworthiness and faithfulness, leads the pure in heart to say, "Here am I, O God, do with me what you will, for your will is good."

God gives the person attached to Him a heart of gratitude, a heart that beats with passion, lives in intimacy, and walks in integrity. This relationship leads the psalmist to say, "Better is one day in your courts than a thousand elsewhere; I would rather be a doorkeeper in the house of my God than dwell in the tents of the wicked." (Psalm 84:10) The gratitude has in it a hunger for more relationship and a desire to walk in dignity and humility: "Teach me your way, O LORD, and I will walk in your truth; give me an undivided heart that I may fear your name. I will praise you, O Lord my God, with all my heart; I will glorify your name forever. For great is your love toward me; you have delivered me from the depths of the grave." (Psalm 86:11-13)

The pure in heart live their gratitude out; they walk it in the dirt one step at a time. They "lift up the cup of salvation and call on the name of the LORD" (Psalm 116:13) or live willing to speak the private story of their lives and what God has done with them. Then they "fulfill my vows to the LORD in the presence of all his people" (Psalm 116:14) or publicly live the truth of who God is before others. The private life and the public life match. The idea that a person can bring honor and goodness to a people while his private life is separate from his public life defines insanity and is hypocritical dung. If we miss the integrity God has for us, we miss the goodness He has to fill us with.

Personal surrender—giving back over—sets us free to be God's. We are created in God's image and we have attempted to live without the Image-maker. Surrender sets matters into relationship truth. Surrender liberates us and allows us to accept God's faithfulness to do for us and with us what we could never do for ourselves—set us free to live fully, love deeply, and lead well.

Our God has pursued us in love, with love, for love to grant us life to the full. He paid the price; we had no money to pay. Jesus pursued us and ransomed us from our slavery to insanity, giving us liberation to walk in integrity.

We have a long history of running from being surrendered. We don't want to leave our illusions of personal power, collective power, or egocentric creativity. So we attempt to manipulate God, at our best, by promising to do good, make extra efforts, figure out more, read books of prescriptions and take them, make lists and do them, or merit the next reward. At worst, we attempt to overcome our condition of neediness without God, at all. We so fear or deny seeing ourselves, feeling our condition, needing beyond our own capacities, telling our inner-story, or risking believing. We run from seeing, feeling, needing, desiring, longing, hoping, talking, and trusting.

I survived in conflict. I wanted power and control, not believing that my hunger to be present in relationship with others and God would have any real purpose.

I did not know or believe that all my efforts—"everything in the world—the cravings of sinful man, the lust of his eyes, and the boasting of what he has or does—comes not from the Father, but from the world. The world and its desires pass away, but the man who does (lives in) the will of God lives forever." (I John 2:16-17)

We live forever by what we leave behind in people's hearts that they can treasure and pass forward. And we live forever in a place we were made for, a home called heaven.

LIVING FOREVER IN 2 PLACES

Our surrender initiates our walk on the path we were made to walk. It places us on a quest of life headed toward home.

The pure in heart once craved power and rejected the true life of God; we were dead in our transgressions, laboring against how we were made. We were dead in our sins that rolled up in the wake of our craving control. We were like the walking dead or like caged animals when we followed the ways of the world. All of us also survived like this, not really living, daily laboring to satisfy the cravings of our masquerade for control. We chased lusts and thoughts that we believed would make us whole, or safe, or satisfied. Like everyone else we were, by our very tragic agenda, objects of every thing that pushes against life. We had set ourselves up for guaranteed misery and eventual *Satan's agenda* final condemnation, which is the agenda of the Deceiver.

But because of His great love for us, God, who is rich in mercy, made us alive with Christ even when we were dead in our transgressions—it is by grace you have been saved. And God raised us up with Christ and seated us with Him in the heavenly realms in Christ Jesus, in order that in the coming ages He might show the incomparable riches of His grace, expressed in His kindness to us in Christ Jesus. For it is by grace you have been saved, through faith—and this is not from yourselves, it is the gift of God—not by works, so that no one can boast. (Ephesians 2:4-8)

These words in Ephesians go on to say, as I mentioned earlier, continuing to be written daily, created in Christ Jesus to pursue and do whatever is true and noble, right and pure, whatever is lovely, admirable, anything excellent or praiseworthy. (Philippians 4:8) These good works of creation God designed for us. He fashioned them for us a long time before we ever thought of them.

He has laid out life before us. Will we pursue back? If we do, we will see Him; we will see Him everywhere. When we do not see Him, we cry out for Him and look for Him—for our God is worth the walk, worth the wait, and worth the work. Another beauty of Him, too, is that He does not hide. He always moves in love toward what He wants. He wants us

He wants me

He doesn't give up, quit, or get tired. He wants us and our greater good. Until the image He made is united to the Image Maker, we are not able to see with our hearts who we were made to be and do not do what we were made to do. He wants us, and we can have Him—Immanuel—God with us. The pure in heart see through such belief, and have intimacy with God through daily surrender.

Surrender, then, in God's language is the action we continue to take to receive liberty from the tyranny just like Jesus said about himself and us in Isaiah 61:1-3. Surrender is our one-time and daily RSVP of "yes" to God's invitation to His full life. This daily RSVP of surrender is our response to his invitation to have more of Him and His will. The pure in heart wish to be in a relationship in which our hearts are fettered to Who we have come to trust, for we have seen

obey
listen

Him. In surrender we listen for His voice; we look to see Him move. This listening and looking is where the word obedience originates. In Latin *obedire* means to listen, from which we get the word obedience. Implied in the listening is that our being will follow the words we hear because we trust the speaker, just as sheep pay attention to the shepherd. The shepherd wants good for the sheep. The shepherd leads the sheep out to pasture and brings them home. The shepherd will even lay down his life for the sheep. Our daily surrender, obedience to who we hear and see with the ears and eyes of our hearts, becomes the desire of our hearts. I desire to follow the One who has given Himself to me.

In surrender, we receive good news in our poverty of spirit—the very good, and fantastic, i.e., the kingdom of heaven. We receive our sight, no longer blind to who He is, who we are, and Whose we are. We receive the holding of our hearts, the healing in our brokenhearted lives. We receive liberty from what has held us captive in this world; we receive light, shining our way out of the dungeon of darkness, despair, destruction, or death. We receive God as our avenger and can now pray for our enemies. We know how they will curse themselves, as we did ourselves, unless their hearts turn and are healed. We no longer have to be in charge through survival, making our own revenge or sight or wealth. He grows us into love, into seeing, and into abundance. He even turns ashes into the oil of gladness. He intends, even sees us before we see ourselves, to turn us into oaks of righteousness, trees planted to display the splendor of Him.

In the lexicon of God's language, surrendered is how we begin our life as children, without even knowing. As children we cannot help but bring our inner truths to others in hope. If we are fortunate, later in life the defeat of our egos allows us to have surrender again. We can surrender again, know it consciously, depend on God and others, and daily be initiated into the great quest of the life He has made and who He is.

We can have the life of daily surrender, admitting our neediness, dependence, memory of our past, hopes of our future, struggles of our present, trust or distrust, anxiety or peace, gratitude or terror, love or apathy, and acceptance or bitterness. We submit where we are within our hearts and our craving for full life—our passions, our purposes, our plans, our will to Him. The Will of His passions, purposes, and plans will find the Best Way for us.

The pure in heart remember their own history of refusal and don't want to go backward. I have found refusal to be the human power, ultimately our only "without God" produced power. The irony is that refusal to surrender becomes our way of attempting to fight the tragedy of life and its internal pain without having to admit we are human, need others, and need God. Refusal to admit our true condition and surrender to have liberation of life increases the very tragedy we attempt to protect ourselves from. Our hardness or callousness toward our neediness makes us lose the life we were created for. Refusal constructs tragedy, the tragedy of cursing my heart into isolation where nothing can get to me, including love.

We refuse our need of heart, our need of others, and our need of the Intimate Creator through four offensive defenses I mentioned earlier. We refuse through defiance, shoving need away, rejecting its depths, and our inability to succeed alone. The world refers to defiance as the pride of independence. It is actually the life of Cain, rejecting God's pursuit to bring Cain to himself and God. (Genesis 4:5-16) We refuse through resignation, never allowing life's hopes, life's pains or beauties to move our hearts to the passion that can afford grief, because grief equals weakness. The world refers to resignation as the balance of realistic pragmatism and Stoicistic moderation, not allowing life to get to us. It is like the life of Moses after fleeing Egypt and before he turned toward the burning bush. He attempted to resign from who he was made to be. Moses stepped into his destiny when he dropped the attempt to live in apathy toward his own heart. God unleashed the captive passion within Moses when he surrendered at the burning bush. (Exodus 2:11-3:4)

We also refuse through compromise, giving enough to win, so as not to lose, cutting deals to get the win. Compromise keeps one distrustful eye on the other person and God to see what they are giving, instead of focusing on what I am doing and how much of me is given to God and to what I care about. The world calls compromise wisdom. Marriage doesn't work by compromise. It is full by giving my heart fully, without compromise. Compromise is like the life of Saul who attempted to have the approval of the people and the backing of God, not believing that the approval of God would give him courage to face the disapproval of the people. (I Samuel 15:20-24) Saul lost his kingdom to a man after God's own heart—David, the mighty warrior, good shepherd, redeemed king, one who sought to have an undivided heart. (Psalm 86:11-12)

Lastly, we can refuse through isolation, doing anything to keep ourselves from being expressed as needy humans. The world calls isolation absolute power, rising to the condition of having total control. It requires the utter rejection of feeling, needing, attaching, caring, concern for anyone, including ironically, what is best for one's self. Isolators or cowards will kill to avoid the neediness and dependency of feeling, needing, desiring, longing, and hoping. Cowards despise love, if one could say they care that much, and yet they will "use" love as a means to an end for protection of survival. Judas committed suicide to stop himself from crying out, to have power over his own need to be forgiven by the One he had betrayed. Isolation is the greatest restriction against our hearts and the ultimate human power. (Matthew 27:3-5)

Refusal of heart costs us our lives, and limits the lives of anyone who would love to love us. The once understandable need to protect our hearts has become blind slavery of our will to keep our hearts locked away in iron boxes.

Our refusal says, "In control. Stay away. I control, I will have no LORD. I need no Savior. I will not feel, need, desire, long, or hope. I will not be exposed. I will not give. I will not attach my heart. I will not. My will be done." And what

---

occurs over time is that my will is done, and I miss God's bounty and lavish grace—all ultimately in a twisted form of trying to have life. I promise you, I understand survival. It can always be justified and it will always give us our rights, and it will always make us miss our lives.

I was already a Christian, but I had locked myself away from the Savior and the Lord from getting all the way to me. I deeply need a Savior and I definitely depend upon our Lord. I also need others and depend upon others, and it hurts. Love hurts. I also need to continue to be who God made me to be, for He has much for me. So I give me to Him, my whole heart so He can give me who I am and who I am made to be. Life is a matter of the heart, and the human heart is made for relationship with self, others, and God. It is by living fully in relationship that we move beyond that time of independence onward toward who we were made to become, and more toward Whose we were made for. Surrender opens the daily process of a lifetime quest.

Only our refusal in its cacophonous rationalizing multiplicity stops us from seeing, hearing, touching, tasting, smelling, feeling, speaking, and having life and having it to the full. The pure in heart see God. The refusers run from even hearing Him.

Easy to say, now; still a lifetime to do, and it, at least for me, is done clumsily. Nevertheless, whether I begin at twenty, or surrender now at life's last breath as the thief on the cross beside Jesus, God's life is now. And that fullness of life starts within the defeat of my will, leads to admission of powerlessness, turns into surrender of heart, and spreads outward into full living. Paradoxically, then, we yield, meaning to give way, which produces a yield, which now means to have fullness. It's a growing process.

Once we really do face, grieve, and see that life is tragic, and really do face, grieve and see that God is faithful in the midst of all tragedy, bringing who He is to us, we find out the living, breathing, experiential truth of the Psalmist. King David said in Psalm 37:4, "Delight yourself in the LORD and he will give you the desires of your heart." There is something written on our hearts that our God desires to do for us and with us. It will be for our best. It will fulfill that something written on our hearts. Surrender moves us into that territory.

For years after leaving our hometown, where Sonya and I grew up, I had planned to return. Everywhere we moved as a couple or where I had moved individually prior to marriage, I did so with the plan to return to my hometown. Everywhere we lived, I had treated in my heart as settling in for a long visit or an extended adventure. I had survived by never fully being present or attaching.

I had believed in mattering and belonging in my hometown. I had memories, attachments to places and people, whether I could communicate these loves and dependencies or not. I had some sort of general plan about how life would be better there, some idealized version of Christmas, July 4th, Easter, Saturdays, Fall, Winter, Spring and Summer. I once dreamed and hoped and believed there. I held my heart back from everywhere we went and from everyone I met with the plan to go home. If I could finish up all this stuff, then I could go home where I would one day really live. I could postpone living, attaching, building things to last, caring completely, giving my heart completely to people, places, and causes until I moved back. This fantasy kept me safe, but I missed the good. Heck, until I got hope back in 1989, I could barely attach to Sonya. My refusals and its consequences, I'm still sorry about.

But I found something out. There are a multitude of nuances and complexities to figuring life out in survival mode. There is only one movement to having life and having it to the full. Surrender: being in relationship with God, Him leading, me in conversation, relationship with others as a cooperative equal, and relationship with my own pre-design of depending and God-greatness.

In surrender, I began to attach. This long-held plan, the fantasy that would fix things and make me whole, I began to hand over. Over the next few years, I moved toward living completely with Sonya, Tennyson, and William in our home in Texas. God gave me great grace and peace to let my heart find a home in Texas, to live well where I was. I even surrendered enough to see living in Texas last. The PhD was finished, I was licensed in Texas. We had careers, a home we had built, a spiritual community; I had dug in to Bent Tree Counseling Center, which I helped Golla start in Dallas. The boys were becoming ensconced in playgroup, preschool, soccer teams; Sonya and I met with other couples, and had cookouts. I had friends. I even began to imagine the idea of vacations in which we didn't go to Murfreesboro. I stepped more into being a man with Sonya, learning how to love. I moved more into being a Dad of heart. I had begun to root myself, digging in.

As I grew, my practice as a therapist in Dallas thrived. I worked mainly with men, their professions, their marriages, their wounds, hopes, dreams, losses, fears, addictions, and longings. I had even done a couple of men's retreats, and was featured for a two-week segment on a national Christian broadcast.

I was growing from the inside out, standing up on the inside through surrender of my heart's substance to Jesus. Frankly, God's daily mercies became my strength and my faith in Him became my courage. Seeking Him became my wisdom. Listening for Him and seeing Him in His word, other people, prayer, circumstances, and illumination showed me that God was doing for me what I could not do for myself—daily.

As I read this, I could say of myself, "Well, looks like he finally became an adult and placed childish things away— you know, maturity." Well, I did mature, but I didn't become an adult. I grew. I did not place childish things away; in fact, I began to come to God as a child of His, so that the childishness could end. Childishness comes from demanding that I be able to do life independent of any other influences but my own design. Truth is, my survival mechanisms began to die out or slough off like snakeskin.

My heart deepened in desire. I began to become more and more a man of heart, more accepting of needs and neediness, more full of desiring what is good, true, noble, right, just, lovely, praiseworthy, admirable and excellent. I longed for life, and hoped much. I began to develop the Spiritual Root System, an assimilation of reading, listening, being taught, and believing how we are created to live and how we can miss our lives, if we do not bury the roots of our hearts in God's soil.

My heart deepened in desire. My spiritual ears became tuned in to passion, and I began to see a future bigger than my own eyes. I saw others through the eyes of passion and mercy, also. Paul prayed that the eyes of our hearts would be enlightened so that we would know the hope to which he has called us, the riches of his glorious inheritance in the saints, and his incomparably great power for us who believe. (Ephesians 1:18-19) My destiny was before Him and His call for me to trust His goodness was likewise in my chest. He made us with a destiny and to trust. He also has for us more than we can ask or imagine.

This deep desire to move back to Tennessee would come up occasionally and I would resettle the issue as unfinished business, unresolved grief, childhood wishes, psychological defenses, caretaking of my parents, spiritual immaturity, distrust in God, and unwillingness to become an adult. Then I would get back to making a home with my family:

Christmases, Easter egg hunts, soccer and baseball teams, playing on the abandoned farmland behind our house, cookouts, trips to the zoo, building a fort from scrap wood, playing ball in the backyard—all good stuff, no doubt. I also worked hard building a practice and a counseling center that grew fast with an excellent reputation of meeting people at their point of need. I lived amazed at what God was doing and felt compelled to press on toward what I was getting to do.

I remember one morning when I prepared to head in to Dallas (some mornings I started the practice day as early as 6:30 am) and Tennyson was standing on the counter where I had lifted him to say goodbye. He stood at eye level to me in his pajamas. I said, "I will see you tonight." The kitchen clock ticked in the early morning quiet. Tennyson said, "Don't you love me?" in the only way a child can speak—pure and true without a grasp of compromise, no resignation, open to needing, without defiance, completely exposed, and no isolation of heart.

I felt a wave of sadness, understanding and confusion roll up inside me. I looked at him and told him that I loved him and would return. I knew that he didn't understand time, work, the world, profession, service, money, bills, responsibility, choices, reality, tragedy, and the rejection of grace by Adam and Eve that left us stranded, but for our cry out and our rescue.

I felt sadness about life itself. I knew that I "had" to leave. I understood how the world worked, and I understood quite a bit about life. But I grasped a question in my confusion.

"What's missing in the good life or the good-enough life I lived? Something is off, and yet this is how life is, true?"

I didn't know how to answer my confusion but to experience it and feel it and surrender it. I did know that I had a promise to keep. I would return, God willing, and I did (and do) love him. I hugged Tennyson tightly as Sonya walked into the kitchen. I hugged Sonya, thankful she was with Tennyson and William, who was still asleep, and then left.

How we leave and how we return and what we do in between all matter. We were created to show up emotionally and spiritually in all facets, to live our lives with others.

Four years of maturing, growing, and deepening passed. There I stood in the midst of my life as you sit or stand in your own. Here it came again. The dream picture, the deeper desirous imaginings of my heart continued to come back; the desire to move back to our hometown bumped against my resolve to settle in, to be mature, and adult. I had always dreamed of such, but that was thirteen years ago now. I had decided God's limitations again. I did not yet believe in the depths of God's daily graciousness or the fullness of His detailed, far-reaching design in His desire for us. I did not yet believe more fully in His timing.

I did not know in my heart that the following words were specifically written for me and you to cling to and hold as true, to remember in the crooked trails up the mountains of our lives:

For you created my inmost being; you knit me together in my mother's womb. I praise you because I am fearfully and wonderfully made; your works are wonderful, I know that full well. My frame was not hidden from you, when I was made in the secret place. When I was woven together in the depths of the earth, your eyes saw my unformed body. All the days ordained for me were written in your book before one of them came to be. (Psalm 139:13-16)

These words are for us, the surrendered, and for the "refused," if they will accept them. How much do we miss in our refusal to answer the question, "Where are you?" (Genesis 3:9)

God said to me, as He continues to say to us all, "Where are you?" I responded, "This picture is deep in me, Lord, you have my whole heart, you know." He said, "Is this you?" holding up the imaginings of my heart to me. God said in Psalm 37:4, "Delight yourself in the LORD and he will give you the desires of your heart." I was being introduced to the difference between wishing and fantasy as stagnation, and passion and vision as a whole other movement. I continued to answer the question of someone who loves me and wants to have me no matter what: "Where are you?" This question brings us to discovering intimacy with God. That intimacy led me to learn much later that we grow into saying, "Here am I, Lord," with open desire and willingness. Not yet, though. I just kept answering the question.

I also began to believe and see that the deeper we go into the depths of who God made us to be, the closer we move into doing what we were made for. And moving closer involves not knowing so much as believing, not seeing, but imagining, not touching, but stepping. Wishing stops when the wind blows hard because it is feathery and weightless and disappears like wisps of smoke. Fantasies are pictures we develop to escape the pain of where we are, and what we feel. Wishing and fantasy reduce us to remaining childish. Passion and vision are things we have, things we believe and bear the image of within us. Passion and vision become what we cannot stop looking for, in spite of the pain. My heart could not get away from my hope, nor my imagining, which was growing into passion and vision. The eleventh chapter of Hebrews more aptly calls passion and vision faith. The writer talks about a great group of people, a panoply of heroes, who had passion and vision. He says, "Now faith is being sure of what we hope for and certain of what we do not see. This is what the ancients were commended for." (Hebrews 11:1) I had a passion and a vision, not a wish and a fantasy. I was growing sure of what I hoped for and certain of what I did not see. In trying not to be childish, I had still not become childlike. In my attempt to become faithful as a man, I had not yet discovered that having passion and vision makes faith in the man.

Jesus said, "I tell you the truth, anyone who will not receive the kingdom of God like a little child will never enter it." (Mark 10:15) God calls to us to trust Him with ourselves, the whole unvarnished substance of our hearts, our feelings, needs, desires, longings, hope, and imaginings. In so doing, He can show us who we are, so we can do what we are made to do. He desires our best, no matter how the circumstances look.

Of course, I did not yet have much of a grasp on the differences. At the time, I would say I still lived closer to wishing and fantasy than passion and vision. However, birthed and growing within me was a continued willingness to experience the difference.

I spoke to Sonya one weekend morning as she was sitting out on our patio. The arbor-covered patio had become a beautiful sanctuary for her. A friend of ours and I had built an arbor of western cedar. We had planted at the front posts wisteria that had grown thick and covered the arbor with purple blooms in the spring. She had placed pots of flowers within the alcove where she could sit, pray, piddle, and think as she looked out over open lands of mesquite trees and grasslands no longer used for farming.

I sat down in a rocker beside her and asked if she would be willing for me to explore moving back to Murfreesboro. She said, "Ok," I remember distinctly. The "ok" was ripe with fear, trust, willingness, tiredness, acceptance, sorrow, wonder, distrust and more fear and willingness. I had never made any major moves without her blessing, and yet, at the same time, I had made several major moves with all the disruptions that moves create. She loved the spot where she sat; she had finally arrived in a place where she had security, even with me. She loved and trusted God, listened to His voice, which I believe is the only way she could have said, "ok."

She said, later, "What if my desires are not your desires?" In a moment of clarity I said, "I do not believe your desires must be the same. I just want to know if you are willing to trust me in this desire?" I was asking her to risk big, with no guarantees, after she had found a spot. She had always wanted to be mother and spouse, a blessing to her family and her people. She asked if I had any true sense as to how much she had already trusted me. "Do you see me, Chip?" she said. "More than ever," was my reply.

I deeply hungered, I told her, to raise our sons in a place I knew and they would know as their town, not a sprawl of rooftops. I wanted them to know the creeks and back roads, the spirit of town, the people who stay, and the place. I did not want to bury Sonya, nor be buried in a place I could not call home. I had a sense I could not explain or prove that I would be a better father and husband and person if I followed my desire to move.

I also, even more hypothetical, had this thought in me that said, I need to go be with my people. Sonya would kid me sometimes about "your people" and sometimes taunt me with her fear. "What people? You think you're Moses or something?" To which I would reply, "I don't know who the people are, just 'my people.'" I knew that my people were not old friends or our families of origin, though I wished for relationship with them all. All I knew were the words "my people" and a dim vision of starting something that created good for others.

Red flags went up everywhere with people I talked to because the idea seemed like a geographical cure for not being able to let go of something or for avoiding life on life's terms. I searched intently and could not find the avoidance. In fact, to me avoidance meant staying where I lived. The idea of moving smacked of impracticality, unnecessary risk, foolishness, blindness to reality, a set up for outright failure, disappointment, bitterness, and loss. Yet I had a willingness to risk my heart on failure in the midst of my fear. The ushering up of the passion toward the vision within me continued to push through the fear. No longer could it be avoided.

We decided to give ourselves until June of the following year to move. The process began in August. I needed to honor the place where I gave my heart and had been blessed, and to honor Golla who had envisioned such a place as Bent Tree Counseling Center. I also needed to honor her as my mentor and to honor those people who had trusted me to walk with them down the paths of risking their hearts in hoping amidst the tragedies of life. That August I wrote in my appointment book, "Move, God willing," on the June 1st blank. I set the date only intuitively because it honored where I was with proper time to dismantle everything. I simply planned some and stepped into what had quickly become the unavoidable—passion for discovery in a vision. I had to go. I could not not go. Our God is not only the God of letting go of dreams and finding acceptance through grief, He is also the God of finding our heart's quest enlivened in our willingness to accept.

Two conversations I had during this time left me with no doubt about the direction Sonya and I headed, even without any assurance of the results. I knew my course was set on the North Star, even if shipwreck stalled the destination. The brain is a tool to make the heart's imaginings come to light. The truth matters much more than reality. God's presence matters more than all the powers in the world. And the ego, our concern for control and "face", stops the true self from finding God's wings.

My Dad gave me a gift during this time. I told him of my fears during a phone conversation. I remember leaning against the trunk of my car, looking down our driveway at the house across the street. I told him that I feared things turning out badly, that if I really did what I felt called to do and what I really wanted to do that I would be punished. Something bad would happen. He told me that the fear was my wounded child. That statement came from the man whose addiction had harmed our family. That love from him and his heart of understanding gave me the courage to discover more of God—"win or lose." Either way things went, I moved forward. I answered to the passion and moved toward the vision. I gave myself to God to do what He would do.

I had no work planned, no home drawn up. I made numerous phone calls, sent out resumes, followed leads, continued to throw my hook in the water and continued to reel it in empty. I had begun to dismantle my practice. Golla, in her graciousness, would not step in between God's call and my heart, though her work and Bent Tree Counseling Center were at risk as I planned a departure to a place with no work and no home. She blessed our quest, knowing full well herself the experience of such endeavors in her own life. We worked together to find replacements to keep Bent Tree growing. My debt increased; my income dwindled as winter turned into spring and the intuitively placed June 1st deadline approached. One thing I knew, by June 1st I would have no income unless something happened. The debt I had already accrued meant that something had to happen, and it appeared that nothing was happening.

Sonya was scared. I remember her wondering when God was going to "get off His coffee break" as June approached. I had gone on a run and stood nearby sweating. She pulled weeds from a flower bed in our backyard. With Sonya, she always turns to flowers; her yards are her canvas. I told her it was going to be okay and I believed wholeheartedly, though I knew good and well I might look like a fool. I also feared that she would leave me emotionally, if things did not turn out well. She pulled more weeds, kind of shaking her head back and forth. I looked at the sky and the ground and sweated and believed God was moving, though I could not see or hear anything.

This moment of living faith would grow, and I would realize something moving within me that became something immoveable later. An adventure we plan with the intent to return. It means to go out and return, to go see in the journey and the destination is the return. The move was not an adventure. The move was part of stepping into the quest completely. In quest, we push off shore into the oceans of mystery because we know that more God lives there. We found that mystery is not the unknown, but rather good we have not yet found. We know mystery to be good because we have shucked secret and shameful ways, live openly to see more of ourselves from others, and have found who we were made to be. The quest moves us into what we were made to do, for which there is no return, nor a desire to do so. Believing God awakens quest.

The second conversation that gave me courage to step forward happened sometime in late January. I do not remember his last name, but his first name was John. John had just become the new VP of a huge consulting firm that had offices on the same floor as Bent Tree Counseling Center. The two men who had established the consulting firm had brought in new blood with John. I had walked next door to speak to one of the founders, who turns out wasn't in the office at the time. I walked past John's open door, and turned back around on a search for something, some wisdom, some kind of confirmation. I had heard him speak for ten minutes on the day he had been introduced into the firm. I asked if I could speak to him for a moment. He kindly invited me to sit down to have what became the final conversation about moving fears and the final confirmation that I needed. He gave me the last gold pebble that turned the bucket over and spilled my life into its future.

Some of you have heard the story of the boy who worked hard without hesitation to empty a stall of piles of manure. He sweated and ached and anticipated with focus. Adults came by, at first impressed with how hard he worked, then worried about heat exhaustion and obsession, as if a child doesn't know when he is thirsty or tired. Finally, someone curious about the child's heart asked what the continuous digging was about. By this time, he had cleaned out all of the stalls of the barn and yet he still kept digging. What seemed beneficial to the world had now begun to be a bother because the manure was gone and the realistic grown people saw no point now.

The boy stopped his digging to tell the curious person that with so much manure in the barn, there had to be a pony somewhere. The person walked away shaking his head in sorrow. He didn't have the heart to tell him about reality: there is no pony. He decided to let the boy find out on his own, figure it out himself, experience his own shame, and discover his own form of hopelessness. Reality is there is no pony, and that reality needs to be grieved. But the truth is that there is a pearl and that hope of discovery will keep a child digging. Adults succumb to reality and survive it by ignoring dragons. Children believe in the truth and can grow up into dragon slayers. Children of God, the pure in heart, press on. They keep digging, face the absence of the pony, and yet continue digging for the pearl, just like the heart is made to find.

John waited calmly for me to speak. His gaze was clear. He had some age in his face and some heaviness in the lines around his eyes and mouth. His eyes were brown and rich like freshly turned dirt prepared for planting. Then, like a child who knew there was no pony but could not stop believing in the pearl, I spilled out where I was: full of passion in digging, but afraid of failure. I told him about my sons and Sonya, my dreams as a dad, a passing reference to "my people," and love for our sons. I told him that if I stayed in Dallas, I had this picture of my tombstone saying, "Here lies Chip Dodd," the dates, and underneath an inscription that says, "He worked." I didn't want to live or die like that. I wanted my tombstone to say, "Loving husband, loving father, loving man." I wanted to live from the inside out and standing up.

I finished quickly, knowing how valuable his time was. He, however, looked like he had and would give all the time in the world. He didn't raise an eyebrow or look away. Then he said quietly, "Chip, my son would be seventeen next month." I heard the "would be" spoken gently, and yet in my mind's eye I heard the crack of wood and something breaking. "He died of leukemia almost two years ago. If you think I would allow fear of failure or pride stop me from moving toward that dream you describe, you would be mistaken. Don't let fear or pride stop you from moving into your own life."

157

But for God's grace, I would have felt ashamed of disturbing him. His tragedy he used as a gift, and blessed me, a stranger, in a moment because I asked in need.

I headed toward heart's desire sure of what I hoped for and certain of what I did not see. I had a passion rooted in my heart, surrendered to God. I had a vision, a picture starkly outlined that I had to go see what colors God would paint within.

We truly are made a certain way, we have a pre-design— and a great Designer. We also have a predisposition to move away from our design until passion and vision ignite us to who we are made to be and Whose we are made to be so we can do what we are made to do. Only surrendering to our design brings us to such freedom in dependence.

Even a notable atheist like Ayn Rand recognized how we are designed to be when she said the following about living:

> Throughout the centuries there were men who took
> first steps down new roads armed with nothing
> but their own visions.

I stepped off the cliff to see if an invisible bridge would carry me across the gulf between reality and truth, common sense and wisdom, ego and self, power and presence, solipsism and dependence, fantasy and imagination, brain and heart, me and God.

I was moving to Tennessee, my old hometown, even if moving required that I paint houses or pour concrete like I did when I was younger. Sonya was with me—though tentatively trusting this "crazy man" of hers. I did not realize yet the depth of her contentment to simply settle in with me, our children, and our home. Where we lived did not matter as much to her as that we lived somewhere that allowed her to paint her love on a canvas called place. I am so thankful that she hoped aloud to God and trusted to step off the cliff with me. God has massive amounts of multiple interventions of living detail all around us if we look and hear because we deeply desire to see and listen. God calls us toward Him, and He is already as close as our next breath.

Five months after speaking to John, we moved. Thirty days before we moved God gave me the opportunity to head up a new impaired professionals' program in Nashville. Thirty days before the move our home sold. Four days before the date I put in my datebook on June 1st, "Move, God willing," we loaded up armed with nothing more than a passion and a vision.

One and a half years after moving to Murfreesboro, I stepped away from directorship of an impaired professionals' program and became vision founder and eventual owner of a very special treatment center. I established mercy and grace and a fight for the life we are made to live as our daily mission for the people in treatment. I decided that we would treat no more than ten people at a time, so that our primary focus remained on the person, not numbers, production, or profit. We treated servant leaders of society, people who had given their hands, heads, and hearts to their dreams and their original compassionate desire to make a difference. Along the journey of their lives these people lost their hearts to addiction, depression, anxiety, and other behavioral destructions. I created a place to help these people recover their hearts by finding recovery from what ails them, so they can have the recovery of the lives they were made to live. For every one servant leader who received recovery, hundreds of people they served would receive direct benefit. I envisioned helping heal and restore, even recreate society one servant leader at a time, and one family at a time.

The doctors, nurses, teachers, pastors, musicians, creators, and visionaries we have treated have all been in desperate need of mercy, having judged themselves, usually secretly, as contemptible beyond repair. They had become haters of themselves and subsequent blamers of others as the only way to survive their own self-judgment. They denied their own true inner struggles and became clueless as to how to ask for and receive help.

The only way they had known how to have worth was through achievement, approval seeking, or caretaking (controlling) someone else's problems. The only tools they eventually depended upon to succeed were intellect, self-will, and perfectionism, or secrecy, as a form of morality.

These people lost their way. They could not find internal security through external means and broken hearts could not be repaired through the tools they were using. I was blessed to be well acquainted with both forms of attempting to find full life in impaired ways. But I had received life, and I was blessed to create a place that allowed me to give away what I had received.

My sons, when they were young, asked what I did. I told them the simple truth that the world tends to marginalize. I help heal broken hearts. I did not go on to say that I work to do whatever possible to help people see who they are made to be so they can do what they are made to do.

I also did not know what people I spoke of when I told Sonya before we left Texas that I needed to "go be with my people." I did not know that God would take the stark outline of a vision and color it in with hundreds and hundreds of men, spouses, and families I have been privileged to walk with through the badlands of captivity to liberty.

Having received unspeakable mercy myself, I rarely stand in judgment, remembering where I was, and where I could return without daily surrender. I also rarely stand without anger, knowing full well that we can have the life we are made for, and we can also tragically refuse the life we are made for by locking up our hearts behind the walls of our own egos. We can imprison the true self away from God and others.

You and I are created as emotional and spiritual creatures, created to do one thing in this life—live fully. But we cannot live fully unless we are living fully in heart in relationship with ourselves, others, and God. This truth is our pre-design. If we live the truth, we see God being God.

So certain is our pre-design that in our neediness, we surrender to how we are made, and that surrender cannot help but be to God. Or we refuse, and the refusal eventually destroys us. Jesus said of Himself that He is the cornerstone upon which all of life is built. He said anyone who falls upon the stone will be broken to pieces: the false self of ego will be shattered and the true self exposed to recovery, redemption, restoration, reconciliation, and recreation in spite of all our failures. He said that he upon who the stone falls, however, will be crushed. If the true self of heart is never surrendered, refusal wins; the person succeeds at never having lived, loved, or led. (Matthew 21:44)

We must be broken to pieces to save us from being crushed. God uses our brokenness as openness, if we reach. People who are broken to pieces and restored to life leave behind a legacy of touching hearts that rolls on into future generations. They have seen God, and hunger for others to see.

I remember a wonderful physician who came to treatment some years ago whose recovery speaks to what I am describing. B.J.'s wife had died eight years before treatment. She had been abandoned, along with their children, through his profession of medicine and through alcoholism. He was a physician of international recognition and former head of a specialty in medicine at a well-known academic hospital. B.J. had always planned to finally cut back and come home, but he had not planned to do so because his spouse of a lifetime had cancer. He took a sabbatical from work for nine months while his wife died. He had peace and closeness, turmoil and despair with a woman he had missed for years and years. She had the same with him for nine months as she struggled to live. He had nine months in the family before she died, and afterwards his alcoholism took full grip.

The man that sat before me, now sober, had a deep baritone voice and spoke slowly. He possessed strength of unknown character captured behind walls of refusal and years of ignoring his heart. He had large presence made weak and shrunken. His face bore the marks of age, dignity, and loss, like nature's cuttings in limestone.

I asked him to tell me about one of his sons when he was young. He mentioned a piece of a story that spoke a once hopeful dream of closeness with his children before "should" ego, denial, refusal, labor, anxiety, and craving set the course of their lives. I asked B.J. what he used to call his son when he was little. The son's name was John. B.J. said, "I called him Johnny." So I asked him to write a short letter to Johnny and then gave him the first sentence:

"Dear Johnny,
Every time I think about you I want to say..."

I invited B.J. to go home to how he himself was made and what he was made to be like, to remember even if remembering shattered him. He slowly said, "I want to say,

'I love you, Johnny.'" B.J. breathed in against a sharp pain, held his breath for a moment and then exhaled the opening of a flood of tears that ran down the crevices of his tired face. He wept and shook with a bowed head in sorrow, contempt, and regret. He saw and felt a piece of the life he had missed which opened the doorway to healing.

I said that you must finish the letter, and I would invite his son to treatment so he could tell John the truth. Then B.J. said, "Please, no," shaking his bowed head back and forth. "I can't, I can't," he said moaning. I said, "What do you mean? Don't miss this opportunity. What would stop you?"

He leaned forward a bit and then raised his head, breathed out heavily as he spoke in agony, "He will think I'm weak." The words sounded like stones of agonizing despair dropping to the ground as his tears continued. B.J. had never heard the words himself, and he had not uttered them. He tried to earn them, and in doing so, had eventually refused to pay attention to them for anyone. Like all children who become adults in the world, he became childish in forgetting his heart, instead of child-like faithful to become a God-made man.

B.J. would be restored by facing what his heart had rejected and missed, and what his son had missed and would likely now reject. I asked B.J. if he were willing. A week later his fifty-four year old son arrived to eventually hear three words that a world-renowned, brilliant, powerful healer had never uttered. This time B.J. would not leave the tragedy tragic but would offer himself to life, to God, and to his son.

After preparation time, John sat in the office across from his father. B.J. read a piece of the letter, came to "I love you" and wept in brokenness when he read the words to his son. John sat still for a long moment, then leaned forward with his head, hands holding on to the arms of the chair. With controlled vitriol he said, "You're too late. I needed that then. I'm grown." Silence filled the room for a moment. B.J. said, "I know," and looked down in tears. Then, the son said, "How could you miss me?" with pained anger. "Didn't you know I needed you?" with anguish on his face. "Didn't you know?" as his body subtly pushed away in an attempt to go away from his own heart. He looked out the window for a moment before years of tears started for him. John hated them as he looked at his father. "I'm sorry," B.J. said, "I love you, Johnny, I'm sorry." John hated and loved the defeat of his own walls being breeched. John then said, "But, Dad..." and tears and tears started for both men as they bowed in their grief and the grief began to move the past and move the future, if each man would keep surrendering to it. The old man stood and the other old man rose to fall into his arms.

Love that is born in surrender disrupts survival and opens the door for God to move existence into life. "Do you and I want to live?" becomes the question. Dealing with our hearts becomes the answer. Emotional and spiritual truth overcomes biology and reality. B.J. had no rights. All he had was his inner man to offer.

Unless we admit our neediness, grow in love and live in dependence, we don't become who we are made to be, and we miss what we are made to do. Then, others miss their blessings, especially the ones who had them to offer. Jesus said, "Unless you change and become like little children, you will never enter the kingdom of heaven." (Matthew 18:3) I am so privileged to get glimpses by seeing through the eyes of my heart what could be on earth as I am certain is in heaven.

Johnny tasted a piece of heavenly bread handed to him by his own Dad who himself had been starved from life by his own upbringing, his own judgments, his own answers, and the world's standards. We're dying every day without ever having lived. The life is everywhere for needy and dependent hearts to receive. Life is not for the weak; it is for the strong of heart.

This "heavenly bread" of mercy and grace meeting neediness and dependence can come from anywhere God and man meet.

One day soon after Sonya and I and our sons had moved to Murfreesboro, my youngest son, William, who was five at the time, had spent some time with his aunt while I was doing some errands. When I picked him up she reported that William had not minded her about some matter. He was then and still is quite the truth teller, about himself and his picture of others and life. He is full of life—full of grief and celebration.

As he and I pulled out of the driveway, I attempted to do the right authority role instead of being my William's Dad. "William," I said, "why didn't you mind Aunt Leslee?" first thing out of my mouth. He said, looking at the dashboard of the car, barely able to see out the window, "I don't know." I asked again, and again he came up with the same answer, what I judged to be an excuse.

As we turned on to the street, I said, "William, I'm going to give you the time it takes to get to the end of the street to give me an answer." He couldn't even see over the dashboard to see the end of the street. I believed like Simon the Pharisee in my rightness, my assessment, my parenting parameters, my rights, his future, my judgment; I thought I was parenting.

As we headed to the end of the street and his doom or reprieve, "out of the blue" he asked me what eight times eight is. I looked at him, his forehead looked a little wrinkled with thought and his eyes seemed genuinely curious. But I knew what he was really up to. He was throwing me off the scent, so that I wouldn't stay on track and he wouldn't face the consequences of his misbehavior.

I kind of wisely smiled and answered the simple multiplication question. Then I turned back to the straight and narrow, the topic at hand; "William, what's the answer to my question?" He said after a few seconds of staring at the dash, as I came to the end of the street, "What's 64x64?"

How did he know my Achilles heel, the place of absolute tough struggle and defeat, where even with hard work, solid effort, my brain could never wrap around the numbers and the "x's" and "y's".

I looked at William, applied the brakes to come to a stop, and said a little exasperated, "William, I don't know," to which he quickly responded, "And I don't either."

I saw in that moment the graciousness, trust and pureheartedness of this precious child who had told me the truth the first time I asked: "I don't know." In the face of getting in trouble, not even being able to see the end of the street, he stuck with love, believing that my question must be good because I, Dad, am asking it, and that somehow Dad just didn't understand. So truthful, trusting William would struggle mightily to find what I could not find, so that I could see what he believed about me.

He gave me mercy, and in his vulnerable and trusting love, he gave me grace. The pure in heart see God, who He is and see Him moving about everywhere. That truth is how come children cry so hard at the tragedy of life and are so befuddled. They "know" God has creation in His hands and heart. So when life doesn't respond like God, they need grown ups around to help them begin to see God more deeply and trust that their tears are not crazy, stupid, weak, silly, wrong, ugly, ridiculous, grotesque, pathetic, inadequate, incompetent, or generally worthless. They don't need instruction about how to control life because God cannot. They need a hand to hold them steady as they walk into life while keeping a heart that will depend upon God in the midst of tragedy. But because most adults are not grown up and don't trust God or see Him or believe that He is faithful in the midst of all the tragedy, we teach children likewise. We assist them in becoming adults by losing their hearts. They then give figuring and being in control primacy over heart, who they are made to be, and God, Whose they are made to be. They lose sight of God. They lose themselves.

People who are false adults take away children's Israel, or their pathway to blessing. In Genesis 32, an incredible story is told about how Jacob became Israel, and received a world-changing blessing; he moved away from adulthood by moving into the quest of being grown up. In receiving such change and becoming Israel, Jacob could become a blessing or teacher of life, instead of a curse or survival instructor. The story goes as follows:

> So Jacob was left alone, and a Man wrestled
> with him till daybreak. When the Man saw that
> he could not overpower him, he touched the
> socket of Jacob's hip, so that his hip was wrenched
> as he wrestled with the Man. Then the Man said,
> 'Let me go, for it is daybreak.'
>
> But Jacob replied, 'I will not let you go
> unless you bless me.'
>
> The Man asked, 'What is your name?'
>
> 'Jacob,' he answered.
>
> Then the Man said, 'Your name will no
> longer be Jacob, but Israel because you have
> struggled with God and with men and have
> overcome.'

Jacob said, 'Tell me your name.'

Then the Man said, 'Why do you ask my name?' Then he blessed him there.

So Jacob called the place Peniel, saying, 'It is because I saw God face to face, and yet my life was spared.' (Genesis 32:24-30)

The word "Jacob" means to deceive. The word "Israel" means to struggle with God. When we struggle, we are present and in relationship, and we find the blessings of life, and we live; with the very breath within us, we move into our heart. Our hearts struggle. We grow up. Roots of our true selves are planted in God, and we grow into fruitbearers. But not unless we struggle and live. Israel means to struggle with God, which takes our hearts to Him; we see Him face-to-face and live.

William gave me mercy. He struggled with everything he had to offer, believing that I was who God created me to be, so he could continue to become who he was created to be. Thank God. Because I could remember my story, my struggle of heart and life, I could see through the eyes of my heart into his love. Instead of denying my own heart of humanity, I could feel and in doing so, empathize with another vulnerable creature's struggle for life. Instead of judgment, I could bring discernment, the wisdom that comes from growing up in heart as a child of God. Wisdom is born in humility, which starts in admission of being human, thus in desperate need of God.

With all that stuff going on when William and I came to the end of the street, I simply said, "Thank you, William. You and I will keep working on all this together."

Blessed are the pure in heart for they will see God. We know our need and pray to stay open, like the "noble and good heart" (Luke 8:4-15) in the parable of the soils; true life in us grows up in the soil that is "open." Out of the heart we may grow fully, and in living God, He is glorified, even in us.

I reached into a ditch to give a heart and hand to B.J. B.J. reached out to give a heart and a hand to Johnny. William offered his heart to me to rescue mine. I continued to offer my heart and hands to others as was and is done for me. Only the needy and dependent receive the full growth of strength and full presence that grace and mercy bring. The God we see does for us over and over what we cannot do for ourselves. B.J. could not see God, but was willing to look. I offered to show him what I had seen. William offered me what he had not forgotten. He knew he was made for heart, for relationship, for life. My opportunity was and is to help him keep his own life through continuing to live out daily surrender to our great and present God.

❧

Blessed are the pure in heart, for they will see God.

One time, Jesus was asked by an expert in the law what he himself must do to inherit eternal life. (Luke 10:26-37) Jesus in his brilliance and penetrating love, asked the expert two questions: "What is written in the Law?" he replied. "How do you read it?" Jesus essentially asked the expert where are you in your heart with the truth you know in your brain. Remember the beginning of this book when Jesus asked Simon the Pharisee, "Do you see this woman?" in reference to Simon's own heart from Luke 7:44. God's first question is being asked again and again and again. "Where are you?" Do you and I recognize ourself in others? Do we see through the remembrance, recognition, and gratitude of what mercy God has shown us, or do we see through judgment? Do we see through the eyes of our hearts? Do we see as God sees? But for His grace and mercy, I have nowhere to go. If others around us do not receive the eyes of a changed heart, they will die alone forever like we ourselves were headed towards—isolation that brings torment. They may be saved for eternity, but unknown on this earth, missing what they could have, others missing what they need, and God not being allowed to give what He has for them.

The expert in the law answers Jesus with the two greatest commandments and the foundation of living life fully: "Love the Lord your God with all your heart and with all your soul and with all your strength and with all your mind and love your neighbor as yourself." (Luke 10:27)

Jesus gave him the points that come with passing a test: "You have answered correctly," Jesus replied, "Do this and you will live." Jesus knew full well that no man could live the two greatest commandments within the capacities of his own human powers. The Law is there to bring us to consciousness of our inability to make ourselves perfect. The law is built to bring us to our need for mercy, for all men "sin and fall short of the glory of God" (Romans 3:23). Jesus came so that admission of neediness and dependence upon His Presence could set men and women free to have relationship as we are made to do. We are created to live fully in relationship with Him, with our own hearts of certainty and with others, because of His great love for us and His indwelling Spirit within us. The expert in the law continues, knowing somewhere inside himself that he must justify himself, or he must face his condition of powerlessness: "But he wanted to justify himself, so he asked Jesus, 'Who is my neighbor?'"

What follows is the story of the "Good Samaritan" (Luke 10:30-37).

In reply Jesus said:

A man was going down from Jerusalem to Jericho, when he fell into the hands of robbers. They stripped him of his clothes, beat him and went away, leaving him half dead. A priest happened to be going down the same road, and when he saw the man, he passed by on the other side. So too, a Levite, when he came to the place and saw him, passed by on the other side. But a

Samaritan, as he traveled, came where the man was; and when he saw him, he took pity on him. He went to him and bandaged his wounds, pouring on oil and wine. Then he put the man on his own donkey, took him to an inn and took care of him. The next day he took out two silver coins and gave them to the innkeeper. 'Look after him,' he said, 'and when I return, I will reimburse you for any extra expense you may have.' Which of these three do you think was a neighbor to the man who fell into the hands of robbers?

The expert in the law replied, 'The one who had mercy on him.'

Jesus told him, 'Go and do likewise.'

Remember, Samaritans were pariahs of the exclusive Jewish culture. A cultured Jew to act in cultural purity would avoid even setting foot in the territory where these impure people lived. They would go around them or pass by on the other side to keep themselves clean.

I believe the Samaritan knew heart wounds, loss, tears, rejection, resentment, revenge, pride and had surrender of all these matters in his heart to God. He had become pure of heart from the inside out, knowing the impossibility of ever finding belonging, or mattering in life any other way. He had come through the Beatitudes; as Jesus said, as the Samaritan traveled on his path of life, he saw a wounded man, "came where the man was, and when he saw him, he took pity on him." (Luke 10:33) He had the compassion of knowing what it felt like to be in need, to receive the salve of healing, and he knew the desire of giving out of what he had received—mercy and grace.

The Samaritan did not give because he had to, but because he could. He did not give because he was more advantaged or of more worth. He gave because he saw himself and he was faithful to the God who had done for him what he never could have done for himself. God had looked for the Samaritan, and the Samaritan had received God. The Samaritan had to have found such compassion from God after he found he could not find himself in his own power. God had made the Samaritan pure in heart. He saw himself everywhere in everyone and thus saw, likewise, the need for God everywhere in everyone. He saw the need for grace, mercy, justice, and faithfulness. Blessed are the pure in heart for they will see God.

CHAPTER
SEVEN

BLESSED ARE THE PEACEMAKERS FOR THEY WILL
BE CALLED SONS (AND DAUGHTERS) OF GOD.

God has great passion for us, His creation. He has great
passion for His sons and daughters to have peace. Remember
that passion is the willingness to be in pain for something
greater than pain. God has clearly shown us who know Him
how far He is willing to go to have us, that is to reconcile
us to Himself, to others, and to ourselves. For God so loved
what and who He had made that He gave His one and only
Son that whoever believes in Him shall not perish, but have
everlasting life. (John 3:16) He sent His son to bring us life
and to bring it, He says, in abundance. He did for us, the
powerless, what we could never have done for ourselves.
He saved us, and He gave us a certainty within our hearts
through His Spirit that life is ours to the full. In this world,
Jesus says, there will always be trouble. But take heart, he
told his disciples, and now us, I have overcome the world.
By trust through faith believers know that they have been

---

reconciled in a life that is broken. He brought us peace, and in doing so, the capacity to live fully, love deeply, and lead well. He brought us a present and a future and a promise to be present in us and with us and around us, no matter what. He has called us in the seventh statement of the Beatitudes to be emissaries of this peace—peacemakers as His sons and daughters. As His children we are called to step into broken places and offer the One who can bring peace.

A peacemaker lives in Jesus' gift of peace or shalom. The word shalom, so often used as a simple salutation, is actually a loving desire for someone to drink deeply from the well of God's living water. Shalom is a word of growth. Its roots reach into the heart of God and feed on awe and gratitude, mercy and goodness. The beginning of the word means to be safe within mind and body, or made complete from within. From the roots within grow the trunk and branches of wellness, assurance, blessedness, friendliness, health, favor, and prosperity. The meaning continues by extending into the natural outcome of bearing fruit—the fruit that comes from being who we are made to be and doing what we are made to do, resolved to live a certain way because of this dependence on and certainty in His presence. Such a little word, peace—shalom meaning we desire the Creator of the universe to have home in the heart of one's self and the other. We have, and desire others to have, refuge and sanctuary.

Basically, peacemakers know everything is going to be okay even when it is not okay. This shalom that Jesus has given us makes us passionate about overcoming the world, too. We are reconcilers, whether in participating in the repair of broken water pipes, the restoration of shattered lives, or the recreation of a broken heart. Whenever we are not reconciling, we need to be replenishing or being recreated ourselves so we can get back to reconciling. To reconcile is to have things be like they are made to be. We live as reconcilers by keeping all things in His hands, not by claiming things in our power.

We abide in Jesus. To abide means to stay and to never have to leave.

In Jesus' shalom, in the Prince of Peace (Isaiah 9:6), we find our lives and have our lives. A peacemaker became so by falling through the doorway of the Beatitudes in his or her past, broken, in need, and lost for direction. We discovered our identities in the kingdom of heaven by meeting the King. We have walked in His presence and live in His presence. He grew us. With His presence, we step back into a fractured world to offer what was done for us and to share Who did it. Peacemakers call out for reconciliation in the midst of life tragedies that isolate us from ourselves, each other, and God.

Life is tragic, and wonderful, and God is faithful to wonderful life in the tragedy. God created life in the beginning not to be tragic. We took ourselves away from God and each other. We even attempted to hide from ourselves, and still do, so as not to feel and face our condition with all of its relational dependence and neediness.

In the beginning, the writer says in Genesis, God created the heavens and the earth. (Genesis 1:1) Lastly, He made us and gave Himself and His earth to us. He gave us to each other, and He gave us to ourselves. We were created in shalom. We walked away. Seduced, yes, but we walked away from the original grace of creation.

We made life tragic by refusing our pre-design and giving ourselves over to our predisposition to grab power. God granted us this predisposition so we would not have to love Him unless we really do. He left us free to choose not to love Him, and thus tragically free to miss our abiding in peace. For love's sake, God granted us power to refuse love, and what we did with the ability to refuse dependence initiated the tragedy of the Garden. We chose ego and will over living in surrender to His love. We chose power over His presence, which is shalom.

God's love toward us has always been about liberty and faith. We can be free of tyranny by accepting who we are made to be so we can do what we are made to do. We can have the lives we are made for only by faith, not by control, as we walk forward toward a place we do not yet see. This very same liberty, rooted in God's love, creativity, and relational nature, leaves us, likewise, able to refuse how we are made. God's love leaves us able to claim independence from creation and refusal of our heart's makeup. This grasp for power fractures the multitude of ways that God has designed for us to participate in His passion, purpose, and plan. Refusal makes me miss the presence and the empowerment of life lived fully.

I related earlier a story about walking into a field one afternoon after school when I was around nine years old. I walked out behind the house through the tree line and out into an open field of broomsedge and fescue. The broomsedge was so thick, it looked like a field of wheat. The field was owned by the Catholic church and school behind our house. I remember lying down in the middle of the field. I remember how cool the green fescue felt against my back through my coat. The ground had already begun to get cooler as winter moved closer. The broomsedge shielded me from the afternoon breeze that brushed over the top of the sedge stalks.

I looked up at the blueness of the sky. I felt the warmth of the sun. I could smell the earth. Then a flock of grackles flew over low enough to the ground that I could hear the rush of their wings combined in flight. Tan, gold, blue, green, black, warm, cool, breeze, whispers of wings, shield, refuge, abiding, sense of wonder, sureness of life, the feel of a child knowing the presence of God amidst the expressions of His astounding creation.

I knew He was here. I knew He was good, that He cares, and that His love, mercy, and grace would always be—for me and for you and for everyone else He has ever made. I walked away from the presence when my life became tragic. I chose refusal, until my heart's craving for life broke through. Who made me was there, had always been, and was just a breath away to overwhelm me again.

As stated earlier, children instead of growing up become "adults" whose minds become grotesquely constructed with lies about the truth. We get good at pretending ourselves away from the dependence and neediness of our hearts. We survive by trying to make our own detached lives. Our need for control leads to darkness, destruction, despair, and death.

We develop skill at conning ourselves away from our hearts, at putting others in boxes (refusing them through our judgment), and at blaming God, who we pretend to like just in case He actually is real. Or we simply just keep moving to the next thing, practicing ignorance at a momentous pace. We "simply ignore" our insides. We shrug our shoulders in denial, breathe out and say, "I don't know." Or we keep pretending to know.

This is the same denial Lucifer uses in John Milton's epic poem *Paradise Lost* when he refuses to acknowledge the creation of God. The angels, in debate with Lucifer, ask him where he comes from. He states that he simply sprouted from the ground like a vegetable. We cannot create ourselves. We cannot fill our own hearts. Alcohol, achievement, sex, success; none of these things can take the place of what gratifies the heart.

If we do not pay attention to our hearts and to the consequences of denial, we can make anything what it is not. Some say that cancer cells in a microscopic slide have an elegance and beauty about them. They do if I disconnect from what they are and what they do. They eat life. They void creation. They kill. Death-havocking movements against the pulse of life's yearning for itself is never beautiful. Life's victory is beautiful. Despair seducing us away from the flame of hope is never good. The fire of hope is good. Destruction crumbling neglect is not awesome. Creation attending to growing speaks awe and amazement. Darkness cloaking anything that blinds the eyes of our hearts is not a blessing. The light that pierces darkness removes sacrilege from taking the place of the sacred.

We are made as reconcilers to walk in light, hope, creation, and courage, pushing back darkness, despair, destruction, and death. These actions are what peacemakers are called to do.

So we, humanity, have wandered very far from where we started in Genesis, and we are not able to return to the way it was. We broke it. Yet God has offered the return forward. He has created in our tragedy a way to find Him, ourselves, and others again. By reconciliation we start with the sadness of tragedy, the recreation of ourselves in the midst of it, and then the joy of knowing that in Christ we are closer to home than we can see. And with His Spirit inside us, we are never alone. We have shalom.

In the story of Genesis, the Destroyer of peace, says, "Did God really say…?" (Genesis 3:1) Implied in that question are hundreds of other rising questions and the beginnings of thousands of fractures that will separate a person from crying out in neediness. "Are you so sure that God is who He appears to be?" "Perhaps your trust is foolish?" "Your belief is your immaturity?" "Your loyalty is forced, isn't it?" "You really believe God loves you?" "Maybe you are just part of a game?" "Are you so sure that God cares, wants good for you, truly loves you, will feed you, or meet your needs?"

Reconcilers daily answer God's first question, the relational question, "Where are you?" We surrender our hearts to God, remembering where we once were and where we are now. Then we press through the Deceiver's trash and move on. We move on into the world where the fractures of the Deceiver persist. We bring the potential of peace through reconciliation because we have refuted the Deceiver's question by answering God's question. We know that life is tragic and God is faithful to keep walking us through the tragedy.

Jesus the Messiah fought to get to us, gave Himself for us, and daily seeks to give us His peace. We in our peace have become passionate to participate in the great mission. Jesus restores things like they are made to be and expands them beyond the limits of what we ourselves can even imagine. The author of life (Acts 3:15) and the maker of liberty (Galatians 5:1) has given us mission as emissaries of life and liberty. Peacemakers are in a war of love against darkness, despair, destruction, and death.

We, the reconciled, are heirs to the Prince of Peace; we are sons and daughters of the great and only God; and we walk as emissaries of the King. We have been given a mission of reconciliation, each of us called to it in our own detailed way. Peacemakers no longer regard anyone:

...from a worldly point of view. Though we once
regarded Christ in this way, we do so no longer.
Therefore if anyone is in Christ, he is a new creation;
the old has gone, the new has come. All this is from
God, who reconciled us to himself through Christ
and gave us this ministry of reconciliation: that God
was reconciling the world to himself in Christ,
not counting men's sins against them. And he has
committed to us the message of reconciliation. We
are therefore Christ's emissaries, as though God
were making his appeal through us. (2 Corinthians
5:16-20)

We live by faith. We live with a passion and a vision. We
live with our hearts up against our sternums, not on our
sleeves. We show up and offer ourselves, imposing nothing
and running from nothing. We see ourselves in everyone,
from the old self who can be made alive or a new self who
can be joined.

Finally, peacemakers have a compelling desire in the
Spirit to live fully, as He has made us to do having been
given life renewed. Peacemakers have a compelling desire
to love deeply, having been loved first by the Spirit who
sought us to make us whole. Peacemakers also have a
compelling desire to lead well, being of maximum service by
giving one's self away for the Creator's purposes.

When my youngest son, William, was eight years old and
Tennyson ten, Sonya and I and the boys were driving home

one Friday night after going out to eat. Summer warmth and early evening coolness had settled down into night. We had had a good meal, and I was just finishing the evening by going down Main Street with my window down and the air conditioning on. The sounds of summer eased through the car as we headed home.

We were sitting at the corner of Main Street and Tennessee Boulevard where we were about to turn left and pass the church I mentioned when this story you are reading first began. Forty plus years have been added to my life since then.

The evening was calm, the day finished. Life was good. I foresaw a vacating of thought. I could pretend, at least for a while, that the magazines and mythology about small towns, sinless people, perfect marriages, and trouble-free living could be true.

Then William said from the backseat, "Dad, do you remember when I hit the homerun at McKnight field?" I heard William clearly but wanted to say, "What?" as if I didn't hear him so that maybe he would say, "Never mind" or "Nothing." Then I could stay away from my fear, difficulties, any trouble brewing, love, and my own son's heart. Since William was eight, not four, I had no wiggle room for imaginative stories like, "Yes, I do remember the homerun, the one that bounced off the top of the car that started the horn…and a bunch of other horns started… and kept going until a hundred car horns blared for hours…and dogs howled…and the game had to stop while everyone ran to their cars in a mad dash…and everyone was laughing…even the dogs that watched the game…." I said truthfully and gently, "No." And then he said, "Yeah, Dad, you remember. I really hit the ball and it bounced over the fence and everybody thought it was a homerun, but really it bounced over, but it was a home run."

I felt more fear and a dawning pain of compassion, searing into my stomach and pulling my heart out. I slowly said, "No, William, I don't remember that."

Children's bodies are barely big enough to contain the heart God has fashioned within them, which is why they need so much care, focus, time, attention, and guidance. God doesn't really see that truth about us changing. He identifies us as children of God and His people in need of Him throughout Scripture. Our bodies only get bigger, and we learn how to contain our hearts. Then the probabilities of having intimacy with God are reduced unless life breaks through. When life breaks through, we can have heart again and grow from the soil of who we are made to be. We need heart food, more than body food. William needed heart food, and I needed to not pretend.

William screamed from the backseat, "Don't say that! Don't say that! Yes, I did; you remember!" The silence in the car weighed in heavily, and a thousand words of heart sat on a tipping point, to be brought into the light or to fall into the dark of unsettled shadows and squashed dreams. My little eight-year-old son beckoned me to meet him in his expression of pain while he was telling me to leave him alone.

The vacating part of me that pretended wanted to run away from William's pain—ignore him or "teach him about life." I had the night planned already. I wanted to fix it by telling him something that I didn't know to be true: "You will hit a homerun next time." I wanted to feel better, postpone his agony by pretending a gushing cut was just a scratch. I wanted to attack what I could not control, shut him down with my own denial about life's tragic outcomes and tell him to toughen up. I wanted to give him a resignation pill—the infamous fix-all—"life's not fair, so get over it and get on with it." This half-truth always works to shame hope into its corner with its back to life. The preponderance of evidence of life's unfairness is always weighted toward loss winning the match. This half-truth squishes hope, makes it look weak, silly, and useless. Most of us do not rediscover that hope in the midst of tragedy. Finding hope, however, in the midst of survival frees us. We are liberated to fight for full life because of Who already fought for us. Perseverance is a refusal to believe that our hero—Jesus Christ—will ever be defeated. Without the hope, we cannot find the perseverance. He called me from pretending to peace. He called me into peacemaking. He called me into the war of love.

I remembered a scene in William's life, some three years before. He played baseball on a T-ball team, the ultimate fantasy game for burgeoning heroes. The player hits a baseball off a stationary tube at home plate and runs. In the world of the untutored, it can be a carnival. But to the boys who can already imagine, it is where dreams can come true.

After a game, William walked into the center of a small circle of Tennyson's friends who would be playing later in the day. He stated stoutly as he looked up into their faces, "Y'all think I'm just a little T-ball player, but I'm not. I'm good, too." The other boys looked at William, heard him, and looked rather nonplussed by the declaration. They looked on, including Tennyson, without comment, question, or concern. And William said no more. It just happened, and I remembered questions rising in me that I didn't ask or move into. "Kids just say the darnedest things, huh?" is where I left the scene.

I also remembered several years later during a pre-game batting practice with Tennyson's team warming up for a game. William's team would play later at the same baseball complex. Out of ten pitches thrown to Tennyson, he hit nine out of the park. The team he played on that year won the Dizzy Dean state championship. Tennyson hit a passel of homeruns that summer and stowed them all in a drawer in his bedroom, with the trophies. He also had a nickname, T-Bone, which became very memorable to other boys and interested parents who are involved in that tiny universe. A universe where identities are conjured up, shaped, confirmed or missed, conquered, and lost. The times were all memorable with our sons, the baseball, the teams, and the families. The boys loved their friends and baseball. William also was watching and hearing and feeling.

We drove home in silence. I cried out in quiet desperation to God about what to do. I hurt inside about my young son. I knew pain. My William was in pain. God said only, "choose." I loved my sons and Sonya. I knew one direction because of this God I knew: stay true to the God who is faithful in a fractured world; stay true to love. Fight for him so he can have himself back and his quest.

We arrived home amidst these thoughts. As we got out of the vehicle and headed toward our back door, I said, "William, stay out here with me; let's sit out here." He said, "No, sir." Tennyson and Sonya went inside. I said, "William, come on."

I sat down where God designed for us to sit. On our back patio, looking out over our courtyard of flowers and bushes was an old church pew. The old wood creaked a little when I sat, having been sat on thousands of times, and then finally landing on my back porch.

I said, "William, sit down." He said, "No," then sat down. He sat in that way that let me know that he might be sitting on the outside but standing up on the inside.

We sat there. Him, staring, full of pain, silent. I, full of pain, scared, wanting and locked out. I reached my hand to touch the back of his shoulder. He pulled away with a message of pain and contempt. I sat there seeing the back of him. He sat staring into the dark.

Then, I said the simplest, most obvious hope prayer I could imagine. "William, do you believe that you have to hit home runs to be somebody?" The question had pureness and powerlessness, trust and hope, wanting and love all over it. Out of deep shalom I spoke into his torment.

Before I knew it, an anguished, guttural cry rose from within my eight year old. "What do you think?" he screamed and then the many tears rushed forward as his torso fell over onto his thighs and his head rested against his clenched hands. "What do you think? All I ever hear is 'T-Bone, T-Bone, T-Bone.' I'm nobody. They don't even know my name!" A wail emerged with chest-wracking tears as his rib cage shook. "I'll never be anybody 'til I can hit a home run." I was leaning forward with him. His tears dropped like rain on the old red bricks, turning each spot black.

I slowly reached out my hand and touched his shoulder blade and his body melted against my leg as I leaned over him in my own aching love. After awhile he breathed with the tired last breath that is rest for the grieving, and then I said, "William, William. I don't even care whether you ever hit a home run or even play baseball. You are William. Your worth is yours, your gifts are yours, you are your own kind of ball player. You'll hit a home run when it's time, or your gifts will play themselves out in many other ways. I love you for you. You have got to be William. I know you want to hit home runs. I know you hurt. But you are made to be William."

He just cried himself into silence, resting against my leg with the side of his face turned onto my knee. He looked tired, and rested, and like William.

Some of the words I spoke went into the openings of his heart. Most of them probably just splashed about and evaporated like his tears. But the love wasn't lost, nor his struggle for truthfulness wasted.

He and I quietly talked more. He said after a bit, "Can we go in now?" "Sure," I responded. "Do you mind if I pray?"

I prayed and then we went in. As we entered the back foyer, Tennyson and Sonya, who had heard the wailing, were coming from the kitchen into the foyer, too.

William saw Tennyson, moved to him quickly, put his arms around him and said from way inside himself, "I love you, Tennyson." There they stood, arms around each other, the one who walked in pain proclaiming love to the one who, at the time, walked in victory. Tennyson's cheek rested on the top of William's head, and William's cheek rested against Tennyson's shoulder. "I love you, too, William," were Tennyson's simple words. William had his heart back and his true voice; he knew he wanted to go see his brother. God has made us right. The world is wrong. Surrendering to God how we are made and surrendering to the God who made us frees us from the world with its standard of measurement that uses power and control as its measuring tools.

When I put them to bed that night, I sat between their twin beds, talked about differing gifts, the need to celebrate each person openly, and told them that God would stick with us as we all grew. I encouraged them to keep heart. I didn't know then if they understood any of what I had said. But they did know they were loved inside their own chests. They did know I would show up in their lives. They also knew, without knowing the words, that God had made me a peacemaker, and that I had a passion for them to keep heart.

The next day William and I were coming home from somewhere. I felt close to him and grateful to have been available to him, and relieved that his heart had been unfettered again and free.

I also wanted him to tell me how grateful he was to have me as a father—I wanted to manipulate a magical moment from him so I could see myself as successful in the mirror of my ego. I disrupted shalom.

I said, "William, do you want to talk some more about last night and your pain." In true fashion, out of the mouths of children come straight, unassuming, uncompromising truths—unwilling to participate in the manipulation games of "knowing" what someone wants without them saying it. He simply said, "No, it felt pretty good to get that hurt out last night." I smiled about his clarity, straightforward expression, and peace about where he was; had it been otherwise, he would have said so. I shook my head at myself, wondering if I would ever grow up enough to be so truthful and free about giving up control over someone else's mind and heart. The first Beatitude never ends. I saw myself and thanked God for his love and mercy.

The following summer, William's baseball team was playing in a weekend baseball tournament. He hit a high-arching ball to deep left center that actually hit the very top of the fence and could have bounced in or out of the park. It bounced out for his first home run. I walked over to the dugout after the next batter was at the plate, and congratulated him. I was struck by how clear and bright his eyes were when he looked into mine. He said, "Dad, did you see me run around the bases like I've done that before?" I laughed at all of us at that moment, and said, "Yeah," and returned to the watching fold of dreaming, desperate parents. Driving home, he said, "You know, it really isn't that big of a deal."

A bitter seed of resentment had reached into the soil of his true identity and had begun to grow tendrils: "I'll show them." "They will see." "I'll be more." "I won't feel." "I'll have power." "I must be that." "I must be somebody." "I'll get even." "Somebody will pay." All that determination makes self-will, pride, figuring, and power mainstays in our lives, and eventually makes us blind to ourselves, others, and to God. They will isolate us from true relationships and life no matter how successful we appear to become. The pain of his heart needed to be known and joined. He needed the emotional and spiritual medicine of true relationship. Ambition had begun to feed off his heart's passion, and precious worth was being enslaved by momentary applause.

And I, his dad, wasn't paying attention. I was not running beside his heart. I had just been watching only. Thank God for repentance, recovery, redemption, restoration, and recreation. Thank God that children are looking for clumsy parents, not perfect parents. Our admission of our humanity and God's pursuing and perfect love remain the portal through which our children can keep their hearts for life. But we must have gone through first to let them know.

You say, perhaps, too big a deal is made of a moment. No. Our lives are nothing but where we are in our hearts and what we do with moments. Little things are the big things. The little things become the tasting and touching, the experiencing of God's creation. But this is only true for the surrendered.

If my sons lost the presence of their own feelings, needs, desires, longings, hope, and the capacity to imagine as bearers of God's image, they will have lost heart. Then their identities will be stalled, and years meant for living fully may be twisted and knotted into destruction, despair, darkness, and death—unless they live in surrender. God takes our surrendered hearts and joins with us to bring us to full life, deep love, and genuine leadership. God is the fulfillment of the heart's cry for creation, hope, light, and courage. He brings the antidote to the poison that would make us lose heart. We don't have to drink deeply of the ways of the world that ultimately void our hearts and smother us with regrets and finally self-condemnation.

I cannot stop them from losing heart, nor can I make them keep heart. I can just show up with them in heart. That is what a peacemaker does. Peacemakers experience where they are in heart by feeling their feelings, being truthful about what the intention of their hearts are, or remaining in confession and then giving it over to God and His processes. Peacemakers live in surrender, having found the bounty of such freedom. God does for us what we cannot do for ourselves. He does it. We desire as much for others.

We know Who does it. We just want it and move. God does it. God, then, sets us apart—in the world, but not of it. We are not "its"; we are human beings saved by grace through faith who see that we are God's poetry being written even now into vibrant expressions of living fully, loving deeply, and leading well. Peacemakers started in brokenness of the first Beatitude and have grown into the daily surrender and courage of the seventh Beatitude.

In Matthew 13: 3b-9, Jesus tells a parable about four soils (hearts) upon which seeds are sown (the truth of God):

> A farmer went out to sow his seed. As he was scattering the seed, some fell along the path, and the birds came and ate it up. Some fell on rocky places, where it did not have much soil. It sprang up quickly, because the soil was shallow. But when the sun came up, the plants were scorched, and they withered because they had no root. Other seed fell among thorns, which grew up and choked the plants. Still other seed fell on good soil, where it produced a crop—a hundred, sixty or thirty times what was sown. He who has ears, let him hear.

Jesus then answers the disciples' questions as to what makes Him use parables. Continuing in Matthew 13:13-15, Jesus says that He speaks to them in parables because:

Though seeing, they do not see; though hearing, they do not hear or understand.

In them is fulfilled the prophecy of Isaiah:

You will be ever hearing but never understanding; you will be ever seeing but never perceiving. For this people's heart has become calloused; they hardly hear with their ears, and they have closed their eyes. Otherwise they might see with their eyes, hear with their ears, *understand with their hearts* and turn, and I would heal them.
(emphasis mine)

There the truth exists. Jesus clearly says that when desirous hearts turn in need to be heard, found, and fed, that healing change begins. The soil that produces a harvest of a hundred, sixty, or thirty times what was sown is what Luke calls in the same parable the "noble and good heart," (Luke 8:15) i.e., open and surrendered, who hear the word, retain it, and by persevering produce a crop, or live a passion, for a purpose with a plan.

When I began the treatment center, the Center for Professional Excellence, I began working with people who nearly all of them have or once had all the appearances of success: professional degrees from the well-known institutions with subsequent continued success. Or they had great success in achievement and reward, in spite of not going to the well-known institutions. The success, however, when coupled with determined avoidance of neediness, increases the denial of the power of seduction. These wonderful people who "have everything" are seduced into a world in which their addictions take them places they thought only others would go. Darkness, destruction, despair, and death move to cover their lives. What these people have come to depend upon to succeed, control through intellect, will, and morality or perfectionism, isolates them from relationship. The need for control then destroys them, their spouses, their children, and eventually takes any capacity left to recognize and speak need. Just like me, they have done almost everything to avoid or ignore the admission of surrender.

Egotism, willpower, intellect, figuring, a hard-driven nature, toughness, perfectionism, daily determination, moral agendas, concentration on consciousness, manipulative conscientiousness, "shoulds", pride, independence, trust in one's own flesh, promises, codependence, self-condemnation as a form of motivation, deal making, and interdependence (i.e. relationship as business), demand, contempt, resentment, anxiety, vigilance, isolation, or even over-involvement and approval-seeking don't work in receiving a life that is full with a heart that is gratified.

Dependence and trust does work. People who resist and deny their pre-design and the true circumstance of their lives pretend. The price they pay to "succeed" destroys them. The free gift of life that awaits them, they believe will kill them.

Peacemakers don't pretend. They contend; they stretch themselves tenaciously with a passion, a purpose, and a plan. Peacemakers are reconcilers whose own fractures have been repaired. They bear the scars of healing and have the courage (heart) to go back into the world from which they were rescued and redeemed. They do not go to fix others. They go to offer what God does. God does it; peacemakers give their hearts, their heads, and their hands to live the message of what He does.

Denying and ignoring the voice of one's own heart and attempting to control one's own environment has been the world's prescription for life fulfillment for years and years. The prescription demands that one's own heart be proscribed or prohibited from speaking or condemned to silence. We resent instead of feeling hurt; we work to become apathetic to resist loneliness. We anxiously control or in rage demand to block the fear that is present in us to let us cry out for God's help. We blame and whine to resist the true sadness that comes from losing anything we care about. We have contempt for ourselves and others for not being big enough to make ourselves invincible, instead of feeling the healthy shame of knowing we are big deals to God so we can deeply depend upon His Greatness to make us great. We depress how much we care, hide our vulnerability by keeping our anger from expressing how much life matters to us. We justify ourselves to avoid the need to seek forgiveness that guilt urges us toward. Lastly, we lust as we fill our stomachs, occupy our brains, titillate our skin, and concentrate on our genitals to avoid the surrender that brings true gladness to the human heart.

The survivor mentality and subsequent identity wills the heart to silence and eventually emptiness; therefore, no place is available for true relationship. True relationship begins in dependence and ends in trust; only through relationship do we find our lives and our fulfillment—like it or not. It is only children that know these things to be true until we surrender to its truth again. Peacemakers become children again to grow up into sons and daughters of God.

Jesus said, "I have come that they (we) may have life, and have it to the full." (John 10:10) He says, though, that, "The thief," all that rejects, refuses, or resists surrender and dependence upon God, "comes only to steal and kill and destroy." (John 10:10) Jesus says about Himself, "I am the gate; whoever enters through me will be saved. He will come in and go out, and find pasture." (John 10:9)

We come to the gate because we surrender to how we are truly made and then we come in and go out, tending, creating, moving, shaping, growing—so that life can be drunk from deeply by those who thirst. Surrender starts this process, and dependence continues it.

As a peacemaker, I tell each man who comes to CPE a story that is true, one I have experienced, and one I live. The story attracts and repels at the same time because it calls us to the strength of hope, to the possibility of a way through the mess. It also calls us to the vulnerability of needing help that most survivors distrust or disdain at best, or have no concept of at worst. All peacemakers offer the following story on some level. The story can get a peacemaker rejected quickly, because a peacemaker steps into violence.

I say, "You are the captain of a cavalry. You ride up to me who sits in the dust on the edge of a badlands beside my adobe. Dust, dryness, heat and silence are everywhere except for the occasional screeching caw of a hawk, or the blowing, snorting of a horse. You have been charged with getting across to the other side. You look down at me, just an unremarkable man sitting out in a territory you never planned to come to, and didn't want to know that it existed; however, if you want to have what you need, you must decide to go across or not. Only problem is, all your training, success, abilities, and toughness can not get you across the badlands. You need a guide. You need a servant to show you the way. We need someone to show up and guide us. We can not do this life alone; though every human has his or her own walk to walk, we can not find life alone."

I continue by saying, "While I am only a servant, I know the way—you do not. When you are ready to walk, I will walk with you; when you're ready to run, I will run all day long. You will quit before I will quit because I won't quit. I am giving you what someone gave to me and they didn't quit."

"When you need to go down into the pit to grieve your guts out over exhaustion, losses, failures, and broken dreams, I will sit on the edge and wait for you. When you need rest, you will be able to shut both eyes because I will keep mine open and watch over you."

'When I say that certain water is poisonous, do not drink; wait for the good water. I will not make you, force you, or shove you into what is your mission I will not run far ahead of you—it's your life. If you surrender to your own desire, we will come to the last gulch, crawl up the ancient red dirt and stand upon a plateau that looks out over the endless horizon of your life's quest."

"You will say goodbye, as I will; you run into your life. I slide back down participating in what God has made me to do—walking into redemption with people who have lost their way. Because I have walked with your inner life of heart, you will live in me because I have seen you, and know you. I have seen God's creation behind your walls of control."

I will not say this next truth to most of these people yet, but I know and they will discover, if they take the walk through the badlands, that God is greater than the tragedy of this life. These people are about to move into the presence of God who enters in loving detail into the lives of anyone who cries out.

These people do not know that God redeems the unworthy because He made us worth it. Our job is to need. They do not remember that we have a God who will not stop until He is finished. He is always awake no matter how deep the dark. Our God desires to "delight over us with singing and to quiet us with His love." (Zephaniah 3:17) Years into my own recovery I offer this passage from Zephaniah. I am so grateful that our God wants to hold us, His creation, near Him, and delight in us as He hums the lullaby to us while we rest in Him. The Old Testament God wishes to hold us like a mother in the watches of the night.

Life is tragic and God is faithful. We know His faithfulness only by facing the tragedies. That is what makes God a "re" God. He makes what is deemed to have no value have much value—redeemed. He makes that which has been uncovered, left naked, and stripped of dignity—recovered. He makes that which is made to be and grow, but has been ruined and voided, recreated. He does these "re" things and more over a lifetime and everyday. Replenished, restored, renewed, renowned—all these "re" truths—occur through the initial move called repentance, or the heart of someone turning away from what does not give life and crying out for life instead.

Those who walk in daily remembrance and gratitude see God at work and see who He is, seek His face, and long to be with Him because we are His and to Him we are finished. We are His sons and daughters.

A former patient at CPE and friend, and now a very well-known addictionologist, struggled mightily to find his life. He had come from a home of provision without heart—a roof over his head, three meals a day, education, church, neighborhood, and material things. He also knew he was loved as in "we just knew we were loved." I would ask him how he knew. He would either point to gratefulness about provision or tell me that he "just knew," then stare at me with a flat face, yet with eyes that revealed just a twinge of fear and wonder behind their refusal to need.

He was a physician in treatment for disruptive behavior and addiction; his marriage was in destruction and despair, his wife was neglected, resented, and blamed, and his sons were being tossed aside while being demanded to be grateful because of what his work had provided.

I remember a moment we had together. He was making no progress, but that which comes from following orders without believing—like the difference between a soldier and a warrior. A soldier fights because of what is in front of him. A warrior fights because of what is behind him. He had yet to put heart in his recovery, and therefore, had no restoration of his life. He was doing right; he stood up on the outside, but he was sitting still and frozen on the inside. Doing right is not worth much unless the truth is in it.

I told him what I saw, as he and I wrestled over his life in the badlands. As he stepped out of my office to prepare for the next group, I asked him a question, "Do you remember seeing your father's face?" He looked at me with a bit of a furrowed brow and the same distant eyes, and walked down the hall like a prisoner of war instead of a warrior hungering to be freed from the prison of addiction. He walked past two office doors and turned the corner.

Moments later I heard the sound of moaning and then wailing. I walked up the hall quickly, turned the corner, and there he was. He had stopped at a small alcove where the guys leave their materials. He had slid down the wall, overtaken by breaking grief. He cried hard and said as I squatted with him on the floor, "I have never seen my father's face." He cried and cried there in the alcove with me and another fellow beside him on the floor, and two or three other men quietly and compassionately standing with him and waiting for him.

The father who had provided had never delighted in his son's presence, had not been curious about his son's heart, had not been willing to wrestle with hurt and pain for his son, and had not risked standing in his son's way by claiming him out loud as his son. He had never seen his father's face; he had never known his father's heart, nor been allowed the most normal experience of life being pure and seeing his father's face. His father had never faced his son. The child had become the man who followed his father's lead. Unless the son follows a father with a redeemed heart, the son will remain the father's boy instead of God's man.

The patient went on to recovery from what ailed him to recovery of the life he was made to live. He tells the story of that day to others in the struggle for life. He tells them how he grieved the loss of his father, saw, felt, and revealed his heart, needed God, and found his path. He saw His Father's face, and he has continued to see His Father's face because he looks for God, the way we are made to find Him, through surrender

🍁

Blessed are the peacemakers,
for they will be called sons (and daughters) of God.

We find God and experience God and know God through
prayer, people, His Word, circumstances, and illumination.
Prayer is sometimes even in the sigh of tired needing; it is
our confession of need and listening. Other people are
often the hands and feet and messengers of God. His Word
is the love letter about His pursuit of those He can not stop
loving. Circumstances are the ways God offers us Himself
in the midst of chaos and tragedy, and illumination is the
enlightenment God gives us to live our passions and walk
into our visions.

God is greater than the tragedy of life, and He is faithful to
restore us into the places and paths we were made to live. We
are not made to survive reality. We are made to live in truth.
God will not stop until He finishes. God walks us through
the badlands of our pains, horrors, failures, losses, defenses,
sins, regrets, resentments, mistakes, and shortcomings. He
walks us through the badlands and into the center of our
beings. From then onward, we live with Him in the quest
that is living fully here in preparation to live forever there
when we are finished.

God sees every child as His creation, and every child
as a central protagonist involved in an emotional and
spiritual struggle that will contain ruin, loss, and profound

disappointment. He stands ready to receive each of his creations to make them His again, so He can grace us with peace, passion, and empowerment. Every one of mankind faces life—either becoming isolated in heart, attempting some form of escape from having to feel life, or choosing to surrender to his or her innate need of God and others.

A peacemaker has surrendered and grown up in surrender. As a child of God, this peacemaker has become an emissary with a clear message: God has reconciled all things to life again through Jesus the Christ, the Savior of Mankind, and the Lord of life. Peacemakers have been reconciled to themselves, integrated so that both the inside of the person and the outside express integrity. Their integrity encompasses truth in living. They trust God. They have resolved to walk in belief, trusting God, not themselves. A peacemaker offers what he has to others just as he or she receives and has received from others and God. A peacemaker brings division, the division between dependence and need versus self-sufficiency and self-will. A peacemaker will experience rejection and the joy, passion, and pain of life's great experiences in the care of the Most High.

A peacemaker brings who God made them to be to what God has called them to do. He has set them free, so in awe and gratitude they give themselves back to Him who says, "Be who you are made to be so you can do what you are made to do." We bring blessing to a cursed place. We do this because of Him. We are compelled.

CHAPTER
EIGHT

———————

BLESSED ARE THOSE WHO ARE PERSECUTED
BECAUSE OF RIGHTEOUSNESS, FOR THEIRS IS THE
KINGDOM OF HEAVEN.

The last Beatitude Jesus speaks completes a process of growth, closes a circle, and declares the final words of a war of love. The blessing in the last Beatitude, "for theirs is the kingdom of heaven," is the same blessing that opened the Beatitudes: "Blessed are the poor in spirit for theirs is the kingdom of heaven." In the first Beatitude an acorn has found soil, fertile and rich always faithful to enrich and its roots cling deeply as they grow up. The Beatitudes that come next, each a dwelling and growth place, show us who we are as we move into the fullness of Whose we are. They, likewise, move us into who we are made to be, so we can do what we are made to do. And we are made, in whatever form we are called to do so, to bring light to darkness, creation in place of destruction, hope to despair, and courage to death.

———————

Our initial admission of neediness has transformed into our freedom and compelling desire. We surrender ourselves daily to Him Who is able to do for us what our hearts crave but we cannot gratify without God and others. He gives us life and it to the full. By feeling our feelings, telling the truth about our internal experiences, and by giving this truth to the process of God, He gives us ourselves, to become ourselves, and to give ourselves away. We live in passion with intimacy through integrity. Through the Beatitudes we grow into living fully, loving deeply, and leading well.

He grows us from believing to seeing to believing again, from acorn to oak tree that came from an acorn. We have grown rich in Him. We bow, now as emissaries, in surrender to Him from Whom all blessings come, remembering how we began our growth in collapse. We are rooted deeply and our boughs extend for the display of His splendor (Isaiah 61:3). Jesus said that He was anointed to bring life to living in Isaiah 61:1-3. And He says that we, the healing and living, will be called "oaks of righteousness, a planting of the LORD for the display of His splendor." (Isaiah 61:3)

We are oaks of righteousness, expressions of what God does with His people in their surrender. God is great; God is good. We are in the world but not of it. We are not "its". We are human beings who are His. We have been made righteous.

So, we cannot lose heart for we know that God has given us the truth to believe, a course to follow, and a life to live. The way, the truth, and the life we have found through

His mercy. God loves us with a great passion that Jesus our Savior has displayed to us on earth and continues to do so in Spirit. We have this treasure in jars of clay (2 Corinthians 4:7) that proves God's all-surpassing power has done for us what we could never have done for ourselves.

We, the believers, have received His mercy, and never forget what it costs—the life, death, burial, and the resurrection of Jesus Christ. Because of the presence of God within us, we are and can be hard-pressed on every side, but not crushed; perplexed, but not in despair; persecuted but not abandoned; struck down but not destroyed. (2 Corinthians 4:7-9)

We, the believers, who trust in the LORD, whose confidence is in Him, will be forever blessed. We will be like a tree planted by the water that sends out its roots by the stream. Our hearts drink deeply of God's mercy and grace, faithfulness, and goodness so that when heat comes, our leaves are always green and when drought comes, we never fail to bear fruit. (Jeremiah 17:7-8) He takes care of us in all seasons.

What work do we do to receive such blessing? Jesus said, the work of God is so simple that even a child can do it; "The work of God is this: to believe in the one He has sent." (John 6:29) Persevering in belief means continuing to believe, no matter what troubles come that our hero, Jesus the Christ, will never be defeated. We, likewise, cannot ever be defeated either because of Him. We have been saved in all the ways that word can imply, from healed (salve of salvation) to given eternity (saved for all time). And we know it.

Persecution attempts to void or render null perseverance. The word persecution means to put to flight or run after with hostile intent. Persecution is made up of two Greek words, *deilos* and *diakones*. *Deilos* literally means dread, to be rendered timid, and by implication, faithless. The second word is *diakones*, which means an attendant, a waiter, like minister (dispenser of medicine) or servant. The two words compose a highly dynamic relational battle. The servant or minister wishes to give, offer, repair, do, or make better—that is to reconcile, replenish, recreate, or redeem. The persecutor moves with hostility to make the servant withdraw the gifts. Ironically, the word persecution (*dioko*) means to run after with hostile intent because of fear of the servant. The battle then occurs as follows: the persecutor reacts against the servant to make him timid (shrunken and silent) because the persecutor is fearful of the servant. By offering our story of life lived in the Beatitudes, we become a threat to all the attempts to stop the heart's desire for true life. Persecution's purpose is to press a person away from surrender that brings life and into the void of silence that brings the null. The action of persecution is to press us into refusing our heart's voice.

Remember Saul of Tarsus who became Paul. He was very zealous about destroying the believers of Jesus. He hunted them down to destroy them. He pressed hard because he was terribly anxious about losing power and control. Jesus met Saul on the Road to Damascus and asked, "Why do you persecute me?" (Acts 9:4) Saul then became Paul. In amazing, compelling recognition of the grace he had received, Saul gives up control. Passion of heart for the Savior takes the place of power. In recognition of and to educate us about the grace of God, Paul goes on to write thirteen of the twenty-seven books of the New Testament!

Persecution is the instinctive reaction of the hidden, "refused" heart to the intuitively responsive, surrendered heart. It is the reaction of the Deceiver to keep the bound and blind enslaved and without sight. For if hearts of humans awaken to neediness and a cry out, a reformation beyond any words humans could speak would occur on this earth. God moves into open hearts. Persecution attempts to keep the heart of those crying out silenced.

Persecution is the movement of the anxious and "dreading" to void or render null the movement of the dependent and "needing" that cry out to God for life. Adam and Eve's timidity and silence initiated darkness, destruction, despair, and death. Their refusal to cry out brought us to this groaning. (Romans 8:18-25) And every time I do not live in my heart's surrender of who I am to God and confession of how I am made, I am hiding truth in timidity rather than speaking truth in courage. I shrink my heart or hide my heart rather than speak and expose my heart. Fear that persecution arouses can take us to silence or free us to be in need. Fear is present in us to allow us to ask for help, to allow us to need, so that we can give up control to the One who has control. He takes our neediness and grows us.

Fear of the LORD is the beginning or birthplace of wisdom. Healthy fear, the humble, clear recognition of the order of creation—I'm not big, but I am a big deal gives us the awareness of a need for God, a cry out to God, and an assurance that God can and does and will.

Persecution, then, moves to void creation, the "rightness" or righteousness of how things were made to be and the righteousness of the redeemed who humble themselves before God. Perseverance, or the push back against persecution, means standing firm in the heart's certainty that our Hero cannot be defeated. We do not live in fear. Our fear is in the hands of the One who has overcome all limitations of the world. God gives us courage. We continue to believe and remember God is present and active in our hope in Him, no matter what the external factors. He is at work in our belief. Our belief will search for Him and let us see Him. (See 2 Kings 6:15-17)

We cannot be defeated. The Faithful One promises that we who believe will always be delivered no matter what persecution we face or what attempts are made to void the people we are made to be. We receive deliverance in three ways. We are delivered from many, many struggles, most of which we never know. God shows us the fullness of His mercy and grace, even in our moment-to-moment living. We will not know how many "near misses" we have been delivered from until we fully see in heaven. His mercies of this kind of deliverance are new every day. A second promise of deliverance is fulfilled when we receive deliverance through our troubles.

We face life's troubles and tragedies and persecutions, and our cry out in the struggle grows us into who He desires and who we desire ourselves to be. This deliverance is often called refining, that which makes us more. The silversmith knew the silver was purified when he could see his reflection in the surface of the silver in the smelting pot.

Finally, we are delivered to trouble, meaning we no longer live on this earth. While on the earth, all of our relationships and our creations in it reflect life to the full; the truth is that our lives are but reflections or suggestions, at best, of how life will be someday. Our best love, our greatest creation is but a dim vision of God's heavenly best. Our thinking and experiencing is so earth-bound when times are good that we forget that where we are headed is where everything is best eternally. The great sadness of going home to the true promise land, for most of us, is the part that involves leaving others behind to have to continue persevering. Still, going home or being delivered to the best is to be with the One who made everything and is everything. No more tragedy. Only life abounding in love.

God delivered Moses to Himself just before Moses was completing his own life's passion and vision. He had spent his life longing to take his people from slavery to liberty. Just before delivering his people past the finish line, God said, "No, Moses, come with me." Moses was freed; many of us think of Moses as missing something rather than receiving the best because he did not get to finish his job. Moses received the Creator, and that is the best. Even that which we love reflects only a mere glimpse of how much the Creator loves us, and we will someday love Him. He cares for and takes care of what we see as unfinished.

If we know that deliverance is ours, we also know that mercy gave us this liberation. We were once blind and now we see, dead but now we live. We remember where we were. Therefore, we cannot help but wish for others to see and live, that they "understand with their hearts, turn and be healed." (Isaiah 6:9) We cannot help but have compassion because we have been given compassion.

We are called to provide a place and a language so that others might find belief. We are living, breathing, and moving sanctuaries. We are the place. The language is the experience of our heart's struggles in this life. We stay in the struggle with all our heart because of Jesus. He has shown us the worth of the struggle.

Our salvation and lives are Jesus' offer and His continuing passion. He pursues us to bring us from darkness into light, from despair into hope, from destruction into creation, from death into courage. Our righteousness that He has given us is to become light that moves into darkness, hope that moves into despair, creation that moves into destruction, and courage that moves into death. Someday, when all have been delivered who will receive Him, the tragedy of this life will finally be completely reconciled. We will see all things made completely, utterly "right"—no more darkness of captivity, apathy, and emptiness; no more despair to seduce hope toward the void; no more destruction that attempts to pull creation away from itself; and no more death that consumes and deceives us away from believing and living everything that is life.

Until that time, we who believe live the belief. We cannot help it. We are compelled. It is a passion before it is a purpose. A passion is a willingness to be in pain of heart, mind, body, and soul for a purpose. Without the passion the purpose fades. I have to care to get there. Jesus has liberated us to live and then care.

Our participation remains an opportunity, or a "get to." Our participation is always an invitation, not a "have to." No persecution or force can stop who Jesus is or what Jesus desires. He wins and we have been given the gift of getting to participate. When Jesus entered Jerusalem only days before the power of death attempted to stop His passion to make things "right," the following event occurred:

They brought it (the colt) to Jesus, threw their cloaks on the colt and put Jesus on it. As he went along, people spread their cloaks on the road. When he came near the place where the road goes down the Mount of Olives, the whole crowd of disciples began joyfully to praise God in loud voices for all the miracles they had seen:

'Blessed is the king who comes in the name of the LORD!'

'Peace in heaven and glory in the highest!'

Some of the Pharisees in the crowd said to Jesus, 'Teacher, rebuke your disciples!'

'I tell you,' Jesus replied, 'if they keep quiet, the stones will cry out.' (Luke 19:35-40)

The foundations of creation itself—even immutable stones—will speak out the truth in joy. The groaning spoken of in Romans 8, "We know that the whole creation has been groaning as in the pains of childbirth right up to the present time," will end someday because of Jesus. Until then we celebrate Him who was, who is, and who is to come. We do not sacrifice or suffer. We get to serve, and we have pain in loving.

We can miss the life in living by denying our need and Christ's presence in our neediness, which places us in relationship with our pre-design, others, and Him. As I have stated several times, we can miss life through refusal. We can refuse to listen to and speak our hearts amidst the cacophony of chaotic noises that attempt to drown the truth. We can be persecutors of ourselves. We can refuse to let the truth of our hearts be known, thereby participating in persecution of how we are made.

Persecution, finally, attempts to void belief. Persecution attempts to stop us from wondering, hoping, and being certain. Belief is what the Deceiver moves to steal. Persecution attempts to push into or seduce the heart, God's pre-design, and move us away from reconciliation with life. Persecution moves against the reformation that awaits or is already active in each one of us who believes. We are at war, a war of love for life that must be fought against that which attempts to kill life. Persecution, like cancer, attempts to eat everything that desires life.

I wish to share a few more stories before I close this last chapter. I tell you these last stories to offer you the truth that God is with you right now, moving in your life for love. Please listen and see with your heart. Without seeing and listening with our hearts we are not alive, though we are breathing. His Spirit is about life and can be seen through the "eyes of our hearts." (Ephesians 1:18-19) Believe—at least by wondering if it could be true.

Now, on to the stories. By the way, I do hope that the journey of this book has been a blessing. I pray that the invisible is more visible to you.

I spoke at a gathering of pharmacists from around the Southeast some time ago. I was given a few minutes to speak about my treatment center and about my perspective on treating professionals for addiction. There were some recovering pharmacists in the room. I spent most of my time giving definition of what makes a professional.

I told a story about a man who interviewed three stone masons as they worked. The interviewer asked the first man what he was doing. The stone mason matter-of-factly replied that he was building a wall. This man works with his hands only, so he defines himself as a laborer. He just merely follows the plan.

The interviewer asked the second man what he was doing, to which the mason replied that he was building a wall for a massive building. This man is a craftsman who works with his hands and his head. He grasps the purpose and behaves accordingly.

The interviewer asked the third mason the same question. The mason replied that he was working on a piece of a wall that will one day be a part of a great cathedral where the people will come to worship their God. This mason is an artist, one who gives his heart to something, and uses his head and hands to make the passion and vision of his heart come true. He has a passion, a purpose, and a plan, in that order.

I went on to say that most professionals are actually artists whose hearts have been silenced or forgotten. I told them that at our treatment center we work to bring these people back to their hearts—the wellspring of life (Proverbs 4:23)—so they can serve again from a passion for a vision. I finished, and then sat down. Before I sat down, I had noticed the facial expressions of attention, focus, and interest on many people. I saw the hearts of people rise to the surface of their faces.

The next speaker stood to approach the lectern. He was there to present material on psychopharmacology and the brain chemistry of humans. He was a well-known speaker and teacher, and pharmacy school professor. As he approached the podium area he said, "Well," in a sweet, drawn out, mocking tone, "I'm an artist; I'm an artist," moving his arms out to his side like baby bird wings uselessly flapping. He had squashed about thirty people in the room. I was one of them a long time ago. I smiled a bit, without teeth, shook my head side to side, and wanted to kick him in the ribs to knock the idiocy out of him. He had just knocked the heart out of people, leaving those who were silenced to push their own desires away. He had convinced the eagles sitting in the audience to return to pecking the ground for food like chickens. We are not made to survive by complying with something that is not true. We are made to live the truth of how we are made. Without heart, though, we never rise up and soar on wings like eagles. Instead, we merely survive the persecution of working against who we are made to be.

I also remembered mocking life, heart, and hope myself. I had attempted years ago to walk away from my heart. I had worked hard to stop my heart from beating with hope and to believe only in biology. Doing so made me sick, cynical, sarcastic, a pretender, and a persecutor of my own heart and others.

In 1975, I walked down a shadowy concrete corridor toward an exit into the darkness. I had no intention of returning to hope again. I did not know that my walk was not just the refusal of hope; it also meant the rocks of despair would cover my heart's soil and my roots. I would become hardened by destruction and live in the mangled confusion of the walking dead.

I failed in my intentions, thank God. The child who walked down the sidewalk stepping on mulberries could not forget the sounds of grackles' wings or forget crying when his picture of Jesus broke. And the grown up Chip could not forget the hope of that child. I could not stop wishing, hungering, thirsting, hoping, or wondering, "If just maybe…it could be true." I could not stop wanting to believe. I either was doomed or a rescue would have to occur. Either the world overwhelms or the heart grows. My heart grew because Jesus lives to grow us in heart.

My inability to conquer my own little world opened me to a liberty I could hardly accept. My failure became my strength. My dependence became my courage. My vulnerability became my empathy. My powerlessness became my wisdom. My surrender opened the door to life. My inability to stop looking revealed the pearl. I had been given what the girl who became the sinful woman received in the book of Luke (7:36-50). I had been given my life back.

I looked into the faces of the people in the room at the pharmacy conference. They were attracted to believing their own true hope of life's possibilities. I saw it in their faces, and I saw it in their eyes. I also saw them silence themselves and return to normal when the expert sarcastically mocked the heart's desire and the possibilities of desires. He persecuted me, to persecute them, to keep his own heart silent. He pushed me away to make himself okay. He ate at his own heart with sarcasm, and others suffered.

The story I tell you about my experience at the conference is a small, seemingly insignificant incident; one that can set me up to be mocked even more for writing about it (i.e., letting it matter). That is the point. Most persecution is day-to-day erosion, rather than dramatic, evident movements that make the news.

Persecution has at its core the agenda of silencing belief and the voice of true heart. Persecution hunts to continue to silence one's own heart by silencing others' hearts. It is the power of refusal attempting to overcome the presence of our pre-design and the presence of God.

If the story I just shared with you brings you to thinking that I am a bit ridiculous, then that is how you treat yourself for believing, hoping, longing, desiring, needing, or feeling.

Persecution works through pervasive subtlety, initially, until it grows powerful in the empty spaces of silenced hearts. The man's attempt to persecute me did not succeed. My heart was not silenced. Quite the opposite, actually. The man gave me a gift.

He also offered me opportunity to see how people of heart differ from people of silence. People of heart see people of silence as being in need of a rescue; they need to be rescued from the captivity of refusal and the dungeon of isolation. We have mercy and wish for them to be free to become exposed so God can have them. People of silence have judgment upon others and themselves. They impose themselves against heart to have control. If you and I remain alive in heart, all the resistance in this world cannot silence what Jesus has done. Christians are to draw out hearts, not press in. But, remember, we cannot give what we do not have. Do we live in surrender? Do we know our neediness? Do we act justly, and love mercy and walk humbly with our God? (Micah 6:8) Or are we white-washed tombs of dry bones who burden people with rules of self-righteousness, rather than offering the inner life of God's goodness.

In 1975, I had every intention not to believe anymore, or at all. God has other ideas. I can refuse the truth, be blind, deaf, mute, but these things do not stop the truth. I can spend my life refusing how I am made by the One who made me, to join my heart with His; but my refusal does not change the truth. My refusal only makes me miss the truth. Then, I miss my life and the destiny others could have had with me.

Through surrender to neediness, I came to believe. In believing, I saw. In seeing, faith developed. In faith, I return to surrendering to God to do for me what I cannot do for myself. Our God is a God of a thousand million blessings. Even at our most surrendered, I suspect we still miss much of what He wishes to give us because our hearts so distrust and our egos so control.

I remember one of the old St. Peter stories, about a person getting to heaven. St. Peter shows the person around their new home. He says that all of heaven is yours and open to you. After Peter gives the person a tour, the person says, "What is in the beautiful building you did not take me through?" Peter hem-haws around a bit, looks down and says, "Are you sure you want to know?" The person replies, "You said all things are open to me." Peter says, "Well, come on," sort of quietly. The two go into the building that is magnificent and seems to have no end from where it began. Rows and rows and files and files are stacked and stored floor to ceiling, beginning to distant end. The two walk to a file drawer; Peter pulls it out, and hands the new person the whole drawer. In their hands it becomes so heavy that it has to be put down, and then it suddenly expands. The person looks at Peter, not understanding. Peter said quietly, "In the drawer rest all the blessings you would not take." We who have been given reconciliation look for God's goodness and righteousness in all things because we see Him moving. He cannot do anything other than bless the surrendered.

My "job" now, or my "art" now as an artist, is to have a passion of heart and to walk toward the vision. As I mentioned earlier, faith is what the book of Hebrews calls this passion and vision. "Now faith is being sure of what we hope for and certain of what we do not see. This is what the ancients were commended for." (Hebrews 11:1-2) They believed; they could not not believe. Jesus set us free to believe and by believing we are set free. By believing we also walk in the footsteps of the ancients; the ancients knew the truth was greater than reality. They knew that He Who is in us is greater than he

who is in the world. (I John 4:4) These living experiences
they knew:

> Truth over reality
>
> Presence over power
>
> Light over darkness
>
> Hope over despair
>
> Creation over destruction
>
> Courage over death
>
> Self over ego
>
> Dependence over sufficiency
>
> Passion over depressing
>
> Faith over anxiety
>
> Healing over resentment
>
> Grief over self-pity
>
> Intimacy over apathy
>
> Humility over humiliation
>
> Freedom over pride
>
> Forgiveness over contempt
>
> Joy over biology
>
> Heart over will
>
> Pre-design over predisposition
>
> Neediness as a gift

We who walk the paths of the ancients know that the
Deceiver steals, kills, and destroys. The Deceiver attempts to
void and make null everything that breathes the Creator and

creation. The Deceiver moves to void our experience of God that starts in the cry out, or confession of our neediness, and becomes the belief in His presence and trust in His movements. The Deceiver prowls about to destroy the truth of the lilies of the field because they express in their utter "forgettableness" the irrepressible presence, passion, and power of God. They "know" the list above to be true. Jesus says:

> See how the lilies of the field grow. They do not labor or spin. Yet I tell you that not even Solomon in all his splendor dressed like one of these. If that is how God clothes the grass of the field, which is here today and tomorrow is thrown into the fire, will he not much more clothe you, O you of little faith? So do not worry, saying, 'What shall we eat?' or 'What shall we drink?' or 'What shall we wear?' For the pagans run after all these things, and your heavenly Father knows that you need them. But seek first his kingdom and his righteousness, and all these things will be given to you as well.
> (Matthew 6:28b-33)

All of the powers of this dark world, the spiritual forces of evil in the heavenly realms, the authorities and rulers of death, despair, destruction and darkness move to stop us from seeing the lilies and believing our God who sees, cares, and moves. Belief is what persecution attempts to blind and paralyze.

This last story I give to you is challenging. What I express to you in the following pages portrays exactly what I saw and what I was allowed to participate in over a period of years. It happened to ordinary people like us—"lilies of the field." God showed His tender mercies in a way that anyone who could see would recognize His beauty and be grateful like a child blowing out the candles on a birthday cake, and then the wish coming to sight. Please be patient with me as I sail slowly to this story's destination.

My sons, as I write this, are eighteen and sixteen. Sonya and I have raised them in all the warp and woof life has in it, while holding on to a heart's passion and vision, to live with two boys in gratitude and to raise two men of heart.

There are two expectations I have focused on with them and two hopes I have with them. First, since they were young I have spoken to them the wish for them to climb the mountain of their own dreams. If they dream and climb, I will always see them as successful, regardless of how much they fall. They will see themselves as fulfilled because they went. Anyone who climbs a mountain desires something; anyone who has a dream hungers for something they do not yet have. Therefore, they must walk into the fear of hope and the formation of faith as hurt, loss, anger, victory, and joy become one's companions. Anyone who climbs a mountain will need God and will also have to struggle with wondering where God is at times as He draws them to His true presence, their true selves, and their love toward others.

I remember when Tennyson had torn a hamstring for the second time, ironically, exactly one year after he suffered a tear as a sophomore. The second tear occurred in Oklahoma where he would have been playing a whole week for Team Tennessee in front of scouts from all over the nation. In the second game at his second at bat, I watched him cross first base, pull up, put his head down, and turn with a limp into the grief of crushed hopes and bashed dreams.

No, it wasn't an earthquake in Bolivia or a starving child in a war-torn country. It was just a young man-child at a broken-hearted decision point. As he spent the summer between his junior and senior year rehabilitating the hamstring, college-recruiting day came and went with little fanfare in our house. Two Division I mid-major schools called with scholarship offers. No more calls came that day. An already quiet young man became quieter.

We talked after "call day" while sitting at the kitchen table. Twelve years earlier at the same kitchen table, Tennyson had sat early one Saturday morning. He had just awakened and come into the kitchen. Some moments after sitting still he said, "I was made to play ball," in a dreamy, matter-of-fact way that children can speak. He sounded clear and resolved. I heard him at that moment name the mountain of his dreams. I heard him and said "okay" inside my heart, and walked with him from then on in his heart's desire.

I asked him this new morning, each of us twelve years older now, if he was scared to keep hoping. "Yes," he said, "it hurts." Very simple. And very true for anyone who lives in their heart's desire. Two days later he limped quickly into the room to tell me with amazed eyes that he had just found out that he had been named to Louisville Slugger's 1st Team High School All-American honors. He became one of three baseball players from our county who had ever received such an honor. One of the other two is a professional ballplayer who comes back every winter to work with the younger players. Tennyson and William had practiced with Brennan every winter for years. He himself is an example of a mountain climber.

Eight major colleges contacted Tennyson later with, "Let us know when you play again," messages.

Tennyson signed with Lipscomb University because he believed in the coach, his vision, his character, and the way they believed in a ballplayer's heart to heal and climb again. Ironically, as God would have it, his college baseball will be played ten minutes from my office.

William, likewise, climbs into discovering more and more about his heart and destiny. On a trip we all took to Chicago, we went to Wrigley Field to see the Cubs play. It was our first time to ever go. After the game we went to a well-known Chicago steakhouse. William, seemingly out of nowhere, said, "I love you, Tennyson. If you weren't humble, though, I would not like you at all." He then went on to say that he wanted Tennyson to have all he could have in baseball because he loves the game so much. "You're the best I have seen at your age," he said, speaking like only a fifteen-year-old supportive brother can. William then said, clearly having allowed the thoughts to rumble around inside of him previously, "I want more dimensions, though. I want to travel, explore, write, image consult, be an actor, be a doctor, and play baseball. I guess I'm just multi-dimensional."

In the midst of the laughter, I believed every word William said. I remembered the night some seven years ago on our back porch and his young heart's struggle to keep who God made him to be. His words came from a heart that pursues many dreams. Because of his pursuit of dreams, he has the resulting pain and need. If William chases William, he cannot help but find God. That moment I took as a great blessing because his words came from a heart that, like his brother, is still peculiarly his own. The words came from a heart that lives, not in resentment, but in a hero's dreams of all that God could bless life to be.

The second expectation I had for them beyond climbing the mountain of their dreams is to hold the flag brave and true. This means to keep the voice of your heart alive, have conscience, live honorably, and truthfully. It means to do what is true so you will know when you are false. Living out loud, imperfectly, cannot help but bring us to the need for forgiveness and humility.

In the days of the past, the flag bearer held the warriors together even in the midst of war's chaos. If the flag flew, then the warriors still had hope in having a direction to follow and an action to take. Holding the flag keeps the voice of the heart alive. Living one's standards and confessing one's failures are hard—but worth it— because we are made to repent. It means to stay in the struggle of life no matter what the costs. Each of us looks for another person who lives truthfully, but still knows his or her own shortcomings and vulnerabilities. Still, this person keeps heart. They grow to live fully, love deeply, and, finally, lead well.

Is this possible? Yes. In the name of God I am able to live this life, having been first broken to pieces upon the corner-stone of Jesus Christ so that He could do for me what I would never have been able to do for myself (see Matthew 21:44). There are only two ways in life: finding brokenness which sets us free, or being crushed which leaves us in the bondage of paralysis and the darkness of blindness.

How will I know that my sons live on the mountain and hold the flag of the heart? How will I know that I am in true relationship with them? If they can "hate" me openly and grieve in front of me, I know that we still have each other.

Love and hate are not so much opposites. They are passions that are contending with each other. Love and hate expose heart. Apathy is the opposite of love and hate. Love and hate must be confessed for life relationships and integrity to be maintained and grown. We must have the door of our hearts open for God to come in. We must have our doors open to see God at work within us. So by hate I do not mean refusal and disrespect; I mean confession of heart that maintains our "re" lives. We are continually being reconciled, replenished, restored, recreated, recovered, and redeemed. There is more and more and more of God for us, if we just remain in confession. Confession, remember, means agreement. I agree that I am pre-designed for life. I cannot have my pre-design fulfilled without relationship with God and others. The old saying of, "I can't, God can; I think I will let Him," is daily life.

Our neediness will remain daily life this side of heaven. Life is tragic; God is faithful. The losses of this life are as many as our hopes are large. Jesus came to bind up the brokenhearted, facing life on life's terms. We are made to live fully in a place of heartache, to make refuge in a place that cannot fully be our home. Our home, truly, is in a place our eyes have not seen, but our hearts know exists. To keep life in life, we must, then, keep heart. Anyone who carries heroism within them keeps heart in the midst of struggle. Their lives are lived accordingly.

So, I love my sons best by expecting them to climb the mountain and hold the flag. This way they live their lives fully. I also wish for them to hate and love me openly and grieve and celebrate in front of me, so that I may be with them in their lives.

One who cares much will hurt much. One who gives his heart to something makes his or her true self vulnerable. One who wars for something great will become wounded and weary. Anyone who gives himself completely on the front lines will be wounded eventually. A warrior needs, then, to put his sword and shield down at times, fold himself up on the ground and grieve deeply the tragedy of this life, personally experienced and personally felt. He will also need others to watch over him, be with him, and hold him; to be heart with him when he has been broken by loss.

A warrior—a mountain climber, flag holder, truth teller, and feeler—will experience loss and confusion because they have passion and a vision for something true that is not finished. And God Himself speaks to the warrior, encouraging him or her to fight on, caring for who is behind and pressing on toward what is ahead, even in the midst of confusion.

Elijah warred for love with his God. He faced loss after a great battle—one in which he was even victorious. He saw himself as alone, still oppressed; the enemy still wanted him dead, and chased after him to that end. He ran to the mountains to find a place to hide, escape himself, others, and God. (1 Kings 18:18-19:18)

The word of the LORD came to Elijah who hid in a cave and said, "What are you doing here, Elijah?" (19:9) After speaking about fighting so hard and working so hard and believing so much, he confessed to his heart's pain and loss. "I am the only one left, and now they are trying to kill me, too." (19:10) The LORD said the following to Elijah in his pain: "Go out and stand on the mountain in the presence of the LORD, for the LORD is about to pass by." (I Kings 19:11) The One and Only who will never let you down was present, calling to Elijah, reminding him of who He is:

Then a great and powerful wind tore the mountains apart and shattered the rocks before the LORD, but the LORD was not in the wind. After the wind there was an earthquake, but the LORD was not in the earthquake. After the earthquake came a fire, but the LORD was not in the fire. And after the fire came a gentle whisper....
(I Kings 19:11b-12)

When Elijah heard the whisper in the longings of his own heart that recognized his God, he moved from the cave of his grief and loss, handing himself over to the One who cares, meets needs, sees each of us, and is good to creation with love. Elijah recognized the presence of God and came out of the cave. God said to Elijah that he was not alone; many others were still in the epic struggle with him. In the midst of his loss, God gave him recreation in the destruction and brokenness, enlightenment in his dark unknowns, and a restoration of hope in the heaviness of a grief that makes us want to be somewhere away from the pain of hoping. God showed up in Elijah's pain. "Those who hope (place their inner beings in His hands) will renew their strength" (Isaiah 40:31), for he has spoken to us like he spoke to Isaiah:

I said, 'You are my servant; I have chosen you and have not rejected you. So do not fear, for I am with you; do not be dismayed, for I am your God. I will strengthen you and help you; I will uphold

you with my righteous right hand.'
(Isaiah 41:9b-10)

Our grief that is made deep by desiring greatly and our
passion to live out a vision of greatness will place us in God's
hands. He said, says, and will not stop saying and doing
what he says: "I will uphold you with my righteous hand."
(Isaiah 40:10) The believer—the needy who believes and has
experienced Him before, who stays needy, will experience
Him again. They see Him at work because they look for
Him everywhere—in their circumstances, in their prayers,
in other people, in His word, and in His illumination into
their lives. But those who depend upon flesh for strength,
who trust in men, whose hearts turn away from God, will
not see prosperity even when it is right in front of them.
(Jeremiah 17:5-6)

Do I live the same life with my sons that I hope for them?
Yes. Clumsy and truthful, mistake-ridden, forgiveness-
seeking, passionate, loving, prayerful, insensitive, generous,
struggling—all, yes. I live my life with them and with Sonya.
I know all the way down into my deepest being that without
God, I have nothing and the life I live will be written on
water. I yearn to live fully, love deeply, and lead well by being
in relationship with my own being, God, and others.

So people who have been made righteous are not people
who are better people than others. They are people who
believe in the One who can do and does do for them what
they cannot do for themselves—set them free. Those who

God calls righteous believe and follow Who they believe. They live truthfully—in repentance and in confession. Their hearts depend upon God, and they agree that they need God. Repentance keeps us from secrecy and confession keeps us in humility.

The righteous have renounced secrecy from themselves or others who have need of knowing them or of others whom they wish to know. Secrets require that our hearts be hidden. Secrets steal the emotional and spiritual energy God gave us to live fully in surrender. Secrets begin as a way to maintain appearances but lead to sickness in all of our relationships. They make us sick in heart by eating away at our hopes and our need to be accepted. They lead us to a contempt that says we are "worth less" than others, and they lead us to a self demand to fix ourselves by becoming good or meriting approval through always making up for past behavior. So tragic are secrets that they seduce us away from the solution of God's touch, healing, and blessing because we are unavailable in heart to experience the presence of God or others. Secrets make people isolated in heart because of the fear that they will be rejected or judged, if they are known.

So the righteous may look more mistake-ridden, clumsy, and even sinful because they stay in the struggle of keeping their hearts turned toward Him. This action is called repentance. The righteous do not walk in self-righteousness, which is the grandiosity of "self-madeness"; they walk in God dependence, which is the freedom of "God-madeness."

Let me live in God-madeness

———

Those who have been made righteous believe God. The righteous also live in confession. They grieve well and do joy well. See the Psalms which are full of human beings in recognition of themselves as human before a good God and before a God they doubt.

[handwritten margin note: NEED TO GRIEVE WELL ...]

We need to grieve well because we experience loss more than any other experience in this tragic life—whether it's loss of dreams, invincibility, control, loved ones, opportunities, or even change. Whatever we value, whatever we depend upon or attach ourselves to, renders us in need of grieving. For every change there is a loss, for every loss a death, for every death a grief to be experienced.

Grief brings us to questions of the heart, need of heart (i.e., confession of heart, making known the struggle with God, others, and ourselves). We struggle to stay in trust. Grieving well means feeling our feelings, telling the truth, and giving ourselves to God's ways that bring us to acceptance of life on life's terms, not love of loss. Acceptance brings us to the freedom to continue loving, even though we know that we will have loss and that change is guaranteed. We know for certain that God is faithful in the tragedy that is this life.

Confession renders itself beautiful and desirable when, like repentance, it is seen as a gift. Confession simply means "I agree". I agree that I am created, and so I speak the truth of my humanity in all of its beauty and brokenness to the Maker. It then means that I profess the agreement by speaking the desires of my heart, its cares, delights, troubles, and tragedies. Confession puts us in the hands of Who made us and asks Him to make us into who He desires. And He desires for us to be people of passion, intimacy, and integrity. He desires to mold us into beings who are true through and through—truly human who carry in these jars of clay the presence of a great and extraordinary God.

Through repentance and confession we remain present in heart to continually experience the presence of God or to cling to memory when we have lost the awareness of His presence.

We were made for so much more than this world teaches us to believe. While the earth reflects God's glory and our creativity comes from our image-bearing of God, the truth is that this world is not our home. We live here well by living lives of heart. We can live here well with loss because we can sense the echoes of eternity in our hearts. Knowing eternity and knowing how far the world is from it, increases our pain for those of us who have heart to believe. But it can also increase our passion as we remember the vision of "more God." It is by faith we live.

Those who live in righteousness are a part of a heritage of passion and vision. We are claimed by those people of faith who have gone before us. The book of Hebrews calls them "a great cloud of witnesses" (Hebrews 12:1) who could not stop believing and "longed for a better country—a heavenly one." Therefore, God is not ashamed to be called their God, for He has prepared a city for them." (Hebrews 11:16) The writer goes on in Hebrews to urge us to "fix our eyes on Jesus, the author and perfector of our faith, who for the joy set before Him, endured the cross, scorning its shame, and sat down at the right hand of God. Consider Him who endured such opposition (for the love of us) from sinful men, so that you will not grow weary and *lose heart.*" (Hebrews 12:2-3; emphasis mine)

To this end, called being fully alive, Jesus speaks parable and story, and history, and the disciples document the story to tell us the truth. The vulnerable, open, or needy heart allows the creation of passion and vision within us. This neediness becomes our faith that keeps us free—free to believe.

Does Jesus truly mean that if we admit or experience our neediness or admit our inner experiences—heart—and turn to Him with our true selves, that He will do for us what we could never do for our selves? Yes.

Paul prays for us in the book of Ephesians 1:18-19 that "the eyes of your hearts may be enlightened in order that you may know the hope to which He has called you, the riches of his glorious inheritance in the saints, and his incomparably great power for us who believe." We believe that Jesus is taking us to more than what we see and making us into what we are made to be. He is doing these things and He calls us to who He made us to be.

We believe and persevere. We know the One who has already climbed the mountain, the One who holds the flag of truth, who has no secrets, who is who He says He is and who knows our losses, grieving with us in everyway.

He also waits with us and works with us as He walks with us until we get home.

> Come to me all who are weary and burdened, and I will give you rest. Take my yoke upon you and learn from me, for I am gentle and humble in heart and you will find rest for your souls. For my yoke is easy and my burden is light.
> (Matthew 11:28-29)

The righteous have been made so by Him and therefore stay with Him. The righteous call to others' hearts, so that they can have freedom, too. This freedom, however, disrupts and creates change. It threatens everything that has kept us silent. Jesus overcame everything, so that we could speak into the enslavement of the human heart.

Some years ago a woman entered treatment for a drug addiction to painkillers. She was a registered nurse, raising an eight-year-old son while enduring an abusive marriage to a rager, as much addicted to control as she her pills. Soon after treatment began, very slowly she spoke of having been sexually abused as a child on numerous occasions. She sat quietly after sharing her secret, staring at the floor with her back against the windows in my office and with easy access to my office door.

I quietly said to her, after a span of time, that the hope she has within her for a life different from what she knew was not crazy or foolish. The longing for a life different from what she had always known was not something she would ever get over. And I told her that her addiction was not about weakness or badness.

Her eyes came toward me with a glazed hatred, and then she spoke with contempt for me and against herself. She said, "I would love to slap you across your stupid arrogant face and walk out of this office right now."

I said, "I believe you, and I know you can leave, and I know that the passion you have in you that hates me also hates the hope in you, too. You are not foolish, in spite of all the experiences that tell you how stupid you are to want to live, to want good for your son, to want love. You are made to hope; you can't stop. I'm sorry. There is something better."

She could have walked out, left, and I would have prayed that good would come back to her life. I risked speaking toward her inner pain and hoped it was the wisest time to speak. She did not leave. She stayed. Her treatment was full of brokenhearted, shattering grief. In the midst of the community of others who sought freedom from addiction and the recovery of life, she got her life back. She has the God who has even to this day, not left her nor forsaken her. Her son is almost grown and is a true-hearted young man, as she says, "by God's grace." The rage-filled husband refused change of any kind, especially the kind that took control away from him being able to control her through criticism and condemnation. She found out that there is no condemnation in those who are in Christ Jesus, and she now lives in that liberty.

Some time ago, she called to let me know that she was sending a gift to me that reminded her of the day she almost walked away from her hope. She spoke also of how rich and safe she feels with God and others around her who continue to hope, and deliver a message of hope. The gift was a small-framed picture of a doorway opening in darkness, with heavy shrouds of clouds around it. A light of life glows from the door that is ajar, and the light enters the darkness as an invitation.

The righteous deliver an invitation to the banquet of life. The invitation was written by a King to people who have forgotten in the silent tumult of their hearts where the banquet is. The righteous offer the invitation in gratitude, remembering themselves in their own former condition. We invite others to the hope we once attempted to silence in ourselves.

Of course persecution comes because those who have been made righteous go against the world's standard of silence and chaos. The righteous threaten the Deceiver's agenda to void creation. "Voidition" wars against creation. If belief can be voided, then life as it was designed to be can be stopped.

Thank God, belief cannot be shut down; for there will always be a servant, someone who prays and "looked and saw the hills full of horses and chariots of fire." (2 Kings 6:17) And the servant calls us to believe daily.

Now for the final story. As I wrote about earlier, both of my sons play baseball. Tennyson has just graduated from high school and soon moves off to college and more baseball. William has two years of high school left. Each can hardly talk about not living in the same house together. William said over a year ago that he didn't want to go on any more vacations after Tennyson leaves home because he would be too lonely without him being there also.

Last year on a Friday night, Oakland High School in Murfreesboro, Tennessee, played in a sub-state baseball game with the opportunity if they won to move toward what a lot of people thought would be a state championship for the players, the team, the coach, and the townspeople. USA Today had the team ranked as #2 in the nation. They had a 42-1 record going into the game. They lost 2-1 in an emotionally crushing defeat. Four of the players went on to Division I baseball and notable accomplishments in their first season in college.

In that 2-1 loss, the last at bat for the team, a great kid, struck out with the tying run ninety feet away on third base. After he swung, he dropped the bat and had already walked straight across second base into center field with his hands on his head before his older brother, who had worked his way onto the field, could get to him to hold him. The rest

242

of the team headed for left field, young men devastated by a game that can break a heart. When the coach spoke, all he could tell the young men was, "Boys, I have nothing to say, I can't talk about it yet."

That Friday night we went home in an emotional wrangle. Tennyson had hit a blistering homerun his first at bat; then all the bats went dead until the last inning when a player hit a double, stole third, and waited ninety feet away to score. Everyone was sad. Tennyson went to his room when he came home, unable, unwilling to talk about the loss. Tennyson's brother, William, the kid who used to look through the fence as the "big" eight-year-olds played and yell, "Bust one, T, bust one," sat downstairs with me and Sonya. He cried. William was a freshman and a junior varsity player on the same baseball team.

He had seen the season unfold, wishing to be a part of it, wanting to at least dress varsity to be a part of what happened between the white lines. He said that night that he was dedicating himself to do whatever he needed to do to get Tennyson back to that sub-state game, so he could finish what he didn't get to finish.

I appreciated his passion, and I believed him, even though he was a fifteen-year-old grieving boy, speaking his pain, love, and desire in a moment of facing powerful loss. I just loved his fire. I also found his hope in the midst of a loss, a call to my own hope of heart and my own hunger to dream about the heart's desires overcoming reality. I hoped to see imagination (image-bearing at work) beat the odds. I also loved the brother bond that could easily have become voided years before in loss of heart, resulting in callousness.

Tennyson and William went on into summer, mowing grass, doing odd jobs, and playing summer baseball. Tennyson played for Team Tennessee in Oklahoma in a big interstate series among nine other states. Three weeks after the sub-state loss he tore his hamstring in the second game in Oklahoma for the second time. His dream was stalled again.

Later in the summer, while he rehabilitated the hamstring, he found out through a phone call that he had received All-State honors as a 1st team 1st baseman and later he received the notification that he had been chosen as a Louisville Slugger 1st team high school All-American. He shook his head in joyful amazement and in confusion. The confusion occurred because on college recruiting day, he received only two calls from colleges interested in him for baseball. Injury and lack of exposure took him out of being of interest. Later in the summer, six SEC schools called interested to see him play whenever he began to play again. He just needed to let them know.

Tennyson said about a month after tearing his hamstring the second time that he never truly needed God until the second injury. He said that he was very angry with God and told Him that he would not talk to Him anymore for a while. Sometime later, I don't know when exactly, Tennyson surrendered everything to God—dreams, injuries, desire, fear, and future.

Tennyson came to peace, found more of God, and continued to climb the mountain of his dreams with a second summer of rehabilitation and another missed summer of baseball, skill development, and scouts. I admired his courage.

He really did surrender deeply and looked for God's movement in his heart, as he stayed the course and pressed forward because the dream was still alive. Now the dream was bigger. It was in God's hands. He moved without fear, knowing his passion and future were in God's hands. He believed God had put the desire to play baseball in his heart, so he pursued the loves—his passion, his dreams, working at it in his daily life. Now his God, the bestower and maker of passions, dreams, and daily life was Tennyson's beginning and, he resolved, would be his ending.

William told Tennyson what he had planned. They began to workout together and did not stop. William, a year later, thanked Tennyson for showing him what it meant to really workout, "to dedicate with more swings." William said, "When I would go once because the coach said to go, you would go five times, four without any coach. Thank you for showing me what it means to work hard."

They worked out at the gym, ran sprints with a running parachute, ran stadium steps, threw, and did extra core work at night. They hit and talked. During the latter part of fall conditioning, they stayed late with some other players, all of them hitting a few more rounds, helping each other, and talking. It was also during the fall that Tennyson and William gave it all to God; Tennyson knowing what that surrender meant, and William believing what it meant. After a time of prayer between them, Tennyson wrote some words of believing on a sheet of notebook paper to remind William to remember. "God gave you the gift to play; play like it," the paper read. William taped it on his headboard. Not a lot of talk with Sonya or me about any of these dedications. They were just doing it. Each of them were hoping beyond what they could see and believing that truth is lived beyond reality.

The brothers became best friends with each other because of their heart confession years earlier, bypassing what could have become heart's hardness. At one point during the winter, Tennyson told William that he was his best friend, a most welcomed statement, and I saw William's face take the words into his heart.

Of course they fought like crazy, insulted each other, were unfair and selfish, just like true relationship works; and they worked toward each other, too, with hearts of the Spirit, just like true relationship works. They did these things with two other children of God named Chip and Sonya. At our best, we remain clumsy messes. How crazy we are to deny our need of the One who repairs and restores.

I loved seeing them have opportunity to go deeper into learning a life of hope and being prepared for a future that would knock their hearts about, but not destroy them if they kept the doors of their hearts opened to God and others.

I looked forward to the upcoming season, knowing one dream. Of course, I dreamed of William and Tennyson's dreams coming true. More so, I wanted William to see God bless the heart's hope and passion in a magnificent way. I wanted to see Tennyson's dream become colored by experiences he could see. I wanted to see God at work in a magnificent way in the lives of us common people. Even more, though, I dreamed of the people who knew each other, who looked through the eyes of their hearts to see like Elijah's servant. I dreamed of seeing like Elijah's servant. (2 Kings 6:15-17)

I knew that what keeps us free on this earth, not trapped in the world's bondage, is remembering that God knows we need Him for everything—from breath to bread—and that He has and will take care of everything. Peter, who knew pride and humility, despair and deliverance, reminds us that nothing is too small for God to care about. "Cast all your concerns on Him because He cares for you." (1 Peter 5:7) He hears the needy. He cares about a fifteen-year-old man-child and a seventeen-year-old man-child in the midst of all of life's global tragedies, atrocities, travesties, beauties, and prayers.

I knew also by remembering my own heart's recreation that God cares even about baseball. I remembered after all the years that fill these chapters and your own chapters of life, too, that God loves the color yellow, the smell of mowed grass, meadowlarks, sundown, pumpkins, raindrop splashes, and more than anything because He made it all for us—He loves us. We tend not to love Him. He never forgets us. We forget Him. He keeps asking, "Where are you?" so we can name our hearts' truths, and He can take them to be with us through them. Children know these things, and broken people remember these things. Children of God hunger for a life that is lived fully, in which we love deeply and lead well. We stay away from the exposure of our hearts and miss joining Him with the eyes of our hearts in seeing the greater story abounding everywhere—the one He has written.

I know as a child of God and a maturing man that while God is faithful, life is still tragic. Hope is hard. Faith is a gift and a great pain. Love in the midst of this life is a miracle.

Peter states right after the tender statement of God's care for our smallest matters that we need to be vigilant, for "your enemy the devil prowls around like a roaring lion looking for someone to devour." (1 Peter 5:8) Remember, as stated earlier, lions hunt for stragglers, the isolated, those who drift behind into the shadows. The Deceiver hunts for those who believe through pride, refusal, or ignorance that they do not need God, or they believe that they will need God only if big trouble hits. The Deceiver hunts for boys who walk out concrete corridors into darkness with no intention of hoping again. I had urged my sons to hope, knowing full well that they would hurt for doing so. I needed to be prepared to see like Elijah's servant because I knew the season wasn't about baseball. It was about heart, hope, dreams, climbing mountains, and holding the flag brave and true, walking into grief, living truth, and celebrating victories. It was mostly about trusting God with our very hearts.

The season opener neared. William made varsity, as a sophomore, and would be starting at second base. All of the returning players had hopes. Some paid attention to them and believed them. Some players held them so tightly, they were smothered in pretending not to care; others simply did not know to look for something big.

Even so, the hope that had faded into last year's memories was blooming into this season's possibilities. Tennyson and William would play together for the first time on the same team for a great dream shared between them— sub-state victory and state playoffs. Back yard imaginings had actually moved between the white lines of the playing field.

Tennyson's passion for the game had become a voice to call others to give all they had to whatever talents they brought to the game. "If your game is fielding, then field with everything. Show the next guy. If hitting, then hit. If speed, then do it. Let's win as a team and lose as a team. We work, and what happens is God's." He said these things after a piss-poor day of team workouts with all the varsity players. He asked the freshmen to go outside the locker room. He spoke his heart aloud—this kid who generally led by example, reserved, often quiet, even shy, spoke and called his peers to give it all they had with heart to each other and their hope.

Like I have for years now, I practice the ritual of daily surrender. Upon awakening I spend time with God, ending the time on my knees, forehead to the ground giving myself to Him, thankful and in need. As the season neared, I sometimes found the surrender to be like eating vegetables, which I like a lot. But vegetables just aren't as exciting as the idea of baseball's return, my sons, and spring's possibilities. I wanted to control something. I wanted things to be like I wanted things to be. I even knew that God understood. We don't get in trouble for our joy and excitement. We just get disappointed and terribly hurt along with our desires and hopes. God is always present, though, so we can talk about it. We are made to hope all things.

In the first preseason game, William hit a single that scored Tennyson from second base. It was his first at bat as a varsity player. I thought, "Yes, yes, yes!" The dream season had begun to unfurl into life. Maybe we will escape for a short time the surly bonds of this world and touch the face of God. I forgot that there is no such place as away— only through.

When I was growing up, at midnight television programming would end for the day. Viewing would not restart until six o'clock in the morning with news or some corny local station show. I remember, though, the sign-off at midnight. A jet crossed the sky through great cumulus clouds as a narrator spoke a poem of grandeur, glory, and dreams called "High Flight." The last line of the poem speaks of the pilot's experiences of life's magnificence, being far away from the world, and near God's glory. "I have slipped the surly bonds of earth," the narrator would say, "beyond where eagle ever flew. Put out my hand and touched the face of God." The television screen would soon go blank. I liked the ending of the poem about being so close to God. But when I went to bed I felt lonesome and God seemed far away. Somehow I knew that touching the face of God would take a lifetime, and I needed someone to show me how to live a promise of hope while keeping heart. We can hope and imagine with passion and vision, still facing how far away we are from touching the face of Love.

The second game of the regular season, William hit a hard grounder between short and third to get an inning started. I saw a hitch in his second step off of the plate, then a painful limp as he hobbled over first base. I could see excruciation on his face as he tried to lift his right knee up toward his hip. By the time I brought ice to the dugout, the swelling at the pelvis pointer on his hip was pronounced like a bad sprained ankle filled with fluid. When we left the ball field, I became more concerned because I had to help him lift his leg into my truck. He grimaced as I helped him onto the seat. We borrowed crutches from a friend later that night, and were able to see the doctor the next day. William had a torn gluteus medius, a muscle attached to his pelvis that had torn away from the bone. I shook my head in sadness and disbelief, powerlessness, and anger. The injury wasn't even common in sports—like a sprained ankle, a pulled quadricep, a sore rib, a shoulder twinge, or a flare up of a sore elbow.

251

William stepped into the process of diagnosis and treatment like an injured athlete; he was treated kindly and with the assumption that injury comes with the territory. He was realistic and factual, caring and good.

I was grateful in the reality of William's injury. I believed God, but what was the present God doing? Where was God in this man-child's dream? He had finally arrived. He could play with his brother, and that ability meant more to William than just being on the field. It meant equality, dreaming, love, healing, being a part of something worth the work, and it meant giving up his competitive ego for something greater of which each of us is a part. William had become a part of something of heart, and it was slipping away. The look on his face, the silence, the questions inside of him, all left me knowing the injury itself had little to do with his heart's condition. The injury would heal. What about his heart? Tennyson had already missed two summer seasons with hamstring tears. All I knew to do was show up in the truth.

Sonya put out a call to prayer for her son's injury. A bit of my old shame and ego roiled within me at the thought of being judged for seeking prayer for something as small as a torn muscle. Sonya knew it was about heart, not a torn muscle, and stepped on out. I just wanted care for William. People did pray and cared even through my old embarrassment. People asked about him at church. Several of my male friends asked about him, grimaced as I told the story, and said they were pulling for the boys. Some of them truly were.

William told me that when he made it to the dugout and eased on to the bench, that he said in the midst of fear, "God use this for you. I surrender to You. Whatever this is, God, please." When I saw him in the dugout, tears trailed down his face through sweat, heart pain, and anguish bigger than hip pain.

I called the same man who helped Tennyson with his hamstring and supported him in his character growth. He said he would also work with William as soon as the doctor permitted. Jo Jo Petroni is a garrulous, tough, sparkly-eyed encourager to young men who have character or could have character. He knows athletes like seeds know dirt, and he knows that athletics can put us in life and life's bigger preparations. He had spent years in professional football and had come back to college sports because some of these young men he said, "would still listen." With love and toughness, Jo Jo took a busted-hearted high-school kid under his wing and cared about him. Tennyson told me that if he ever became a pro that he would buy a car and leave it in Jo Jo's driveway. He said he would make him take it because of how Jo Jo had helped him. The man loves character, has it himself, as do his sons.

William began his time during the games in the dugout, waiting, struggling emotionally and spiritually, and encouraging his peers. Three weeks of healing based upon the doctor's initial report turned into six, then seven weeks. The season itself is only a little more than seven weeks. The dream season, the year of dedication, the hopes more and more became like holding air. William fought through bitterness and fears by keeping his heart truthful. I walked with him. I urged him to stay on the mountain, stay in the struggle. I urged him to sit with the flag still standing. And, "You bet I'm angry, too," I said.

Unlike Sysiphus who survived the gods' curse through resignation, I called out and believed in a God who knows our sorrows and cares. Instead of giving up and pushing the stone up the mountain again like Sysiphus, I continued to surrender as a man of heart to the God who has rolled the stone away in a forever way.

God was listening to William. He saw William. He was with William. Even if he missed the whole season, something good would come. What God had done with me, a child of His, proved already what He could do with William. He had walked beside my heart of refusal, and God now held my heart of surrender. I was just an average person, which translates into being nobody in the world's terms. God, however, sees you and me as someone worth sending the One to rescue us. I knew He heard me, saw me, and was with us.

He knew William's heart, his prayers, and his openings. God was doing something. I had no idea if it was for the present time or thirty years from now. I just stayed angry in the struggle and watched to see what He was doing and would do.

One night William and I rode home together from church. He stared straight ahead into the windshield. After some stuffed silence, he said, "What's God doing? If God did this, what for? If He didn't, then why didn't He stop it? If He couldn't stop it, then He can't really do anything, and if He did this, I don't like Him at all."

The short drive home from church ended before William finished expressing himself. He stepped out of the passenger side of my truck and slammed the door, walked over to his car, which is older than he is, to lock up for the night. I got out of my truck and slowly walked toward him to stay with him. He and I stood near the edge of the light that shines down on the driveway from our garage. With a tired voice and a slight smile, he said, "I don't mean what I'm saying so much, but I need to say it all because you can take it. You have something to say and it is not that you'll pray, or say how I should be grateful or how it's okay; 'cause it's not okay."

He and I hugged there, and I rubbed his burr-head haircut. I said, "No, it's not okay, and I'm sorry. I'm angry and something is in this William. God is here." We went inside; more days rolled by. He persevered. He believed his Hero could not be defeated. He struggled.

The team won a bunch of games during the season, cobbling together wins with a little bit of everything, a great pitching outing, a critical hit, and a defensive play that sparked a rally. Tennyson was being pitched around many times at the plate, slowly setting a record for walks, and slowly becoming more frustrated. But he led. He believed. He called all the players to keep on. He began to press, not hitting as well as the year before. Few people expected the team to be very good after the loss of four Division I signees.

He wondered quietly one night at our kitchen table if maybe he was a fluke. Perhaps All-State, All-American honors were a one-season fluke. I said, "If you attempt to defend or live up to some image others have of you, or you create of yourself, you'll forget your love, your dreams, or the work in front of you that lets dreams come true. I know you're struggling, too, you and William. William's not even playing, and you may be pressing too much to make something happen to prove something that already is.

You're a great ballplayer because you love the game, and you're leading in your love. Do you remember the first time you got to play again after being out three months? We were in Knoxville at that showcase. You seemed so alive. You told me what I thought was true; that you were on the field, between the white lines where everything made sense, and you felt the simple joy of being where you desire to be. Keep following your love; your passion isn't a fluke even when it doesn't match what's happening around you or the results. Keep on, son." I told him what I saw, felt, believed, and knew. He listened without comment. He remembered that day at the showcase. He nodded. I so love his quiet tenderness and absorbing heart.

Doubt, dismay, and despair lurked around the edges of my son's believing, seeing, and hoping. I watched him keep growing through the frustration, urging his teammates to give all, win or lose, bring it all. He did—no resignation caught the young man's heart.

The team had a leader—by example, action, and belief. Two summers of torn hamstring repair, keeping passion in the face of difficulty, surrendering to trust in God's presence and plans—whatever they were—brought Tennyson to the voice of his heart and taught him how to keep it.

The righteous bring themselves to God—all the verities of who He is, what He is, what He does, and our heart's certainty in Him (even in struggle)—to where He goes. God's people bring truth to reality. The righteous are sons and daughters of God. They live how they are made and listen to the One who made them.

My sons in the midst of disturbance were staying the course of their own hearts, redeemed hearts. They were staying the course of who they were made to be, as was I. You and I will be pushed, perhaps chased down to relinquish the voices of our hearts. We will be pushed to move away from what we know to be true. We who live the Beatitudes believe in and have experienced the truth of God enough to doubt reality. We believe in the bigger story behind what reality tells us. The righteous by faith stay in the story, and the righteous will be persecuted as an attempt to be chased into silence of heart.

William no longer needed crutches. Little sign of a limp remained. He followed Jo Jo's regimen with discipline. He also studied a lot of hitting and styles of handling frustration and failure while sitting in the dugout. He made a lot of decisions about how he would play, if he got to play.

He would play beyond the focus on a state championship and others' approval or applause. He would play in gratitude, for the team and for an audience of One. He would believe that if he couldn't get it done, then the next person would; nothing but passion, if he could just get to the plate again. He wanted to play a part in something great. More than anything, he wanted to be with his brother between the white lines.

The character of heart that God longs for us He builds a block at a time. Our neediness of God grows character of heart in us. Whether or not it will stand is revealed in crisis. Character is exposed and expressed when the realities of life go against the truth of who God is and the truth of who God made us to be. We are made to hope, feel, need, desire, long, imagine, believe, and love in spite of every reality in this world that counters God's creation and creativity. The truth must overcome reality.

Crisis challenges truth for all of us. It puts us in a position to face, feel, and experience our neediness. It reveals character or the need for character development.

Character lets us lean into the certainty of God being in loving control or the memory of hope of God being in loving control. Sometimes, character means clinging just to the hope of God being in loving control because the foundation of certainty is shaking and the shelter of memory is trembling.

Nevertheless, character, the character of righteousness, brings us rest, trust, confidence, and renewed strength. Remembering and knowing His love lets us cling to His rightness. Our character, our righteousness, is only our depending on His "rightness" or His whole character of goodness, love, grace, and justice. Irony of ironies, or the great beautiful paradox, is that our righteousness circles us back to remembering and staying in our beginnings. Our struggle in life brings us to our continuing to abide with Him through our struggle of heart's neediness. The struggle brings us to Him and deepens our intimacy with Him. "Blessed are the poor in spirit" for our cry out continues to bring us to experiencing His presence. The "poor in spirit" get the presence of God, which draws us to know Him more. We live with Him in the struggle of our hearts.

He shows Himself more. He builds our faith as faith is built in intimacy. He gives us a peace through hearts that are given to Him daily. He builds His "rightness" in us. But we will struggle as long as we live here to depend upon the One who longs to hold us in truth and make us more than we ourselves could even ask or imagine. We are made for His workings in our hearts and for truths to overcome reality. We are made to believe.

William could not get to the place his heart desired, and God desired for Him, without a struggle in the territory of God's ways—ways of the heart, in heart training.

Both of my sons, and Sonya and I too, had been discouraged—questioned the worth and sanity of keeping heart. One Sunday afternoon we sat on our back patio and talked. After we talked about the struggles, heartaches, and fears, the memories of good, and a bunch of other things, some light hearted, some just easy, I said to Tennyson and William something that struck me very clearly like the last mark to close a great circle; Sonya understood very deeply.

"Thirty-three years ago, this time of year," I said, "my own pursuit to be All-State, to become somebody, and more, was over—and in some ways just beginning. I lost, clueless as to any of my desires truly having anything to do with God or true self, ego, what was best, love, acceptance, or whatever. I essentially exited my heart." I went on to say that what God did, even with the ugly results of my exit, through surrender of heart, brought me to them. I could show up in heart with them in this place. I said, "I can be with you and ask the questions I didn't know how to ask or even speak then."

Living the Beatitudes, walking into grasping some of the vastness of God's love for us, allowed me to speak to them about keeping heart, living through loss, and God's amazing movements. I could see them, knew them, and could be with them through my own losses and theirs. If my losses brought me to this place to be with them in their pain, then how much much wonderful worth did all the loss have? I supported them in keeping heart, seeking God, no matter what, win or lose.

"Climb the mountain and hold the flag," I said. They smiled the "yea, yea, Dad, smile" and absorbed the truth. I felt joy in the moment to be a part of their destinies. Every child is made for one. Every child of God lives destiny. Every child of God is protected in and guided in their destiny. The sad part is that we miss so much of the goodness because we do not believe and then do not see with the eyes of God's intimacy. I called my sons to keep risking belief in that moment. I urged them to seek and reach for God to have Him more. Or they could dismiss their hearts, refuse, and not find Him more. We do not live by being away from life. We live by going through life, present in heart. God takes us through, not away from our lives. The righteous know this truth and offer it—never self-righteous, always as God-made righteous.

God says to us, His sons and daughters:

I have chosen you and have not rejected you. So do not fear, for I am with you. Do not be dismayed, for I am your God. I will strengthen you and help you. I will uphold you with my righteous right hand. (Isaiah 41:9-10)

"I am with you," He says; only through our dependence do we know His presence. Even after experiencing His goodness deep into the Beatitudes, we still forget and reject our neediness. Often the last place we turn while yoked to Him is to Him.

William had missed all but two games of the regular season. After the regular season, the team had a district playoff championship. The winner would advance to regional play. If the team somehow made it victoriously through regionals, they would be in the sub-state final—the same place that the dreams of last year's team were crushed and the same place that William committed himself to a God-sized project.

Two games before the district playoffs began, Jo Jo told William that he could dress to play, but he could only play at eighty percent, not all the way. William was both excited and scared. We thanked God, and he went. I was so grateful that William had the opportunity to return to his dream and that Tennyson and the rest of the team had a needed player back to see what could happen. I was hoping big. I wanted to see. I wanted to experience a whisper of His evident glory before my very eyes. I wanted to be there and see it with my own eyes. I hungered for the story to be seen and for it to be known that God's glory which is with us every moment could not be denied this time, unless denial was the goal. I, too, deeply desired to find acceptance in heart through glorious evidence instead of grieving to find acceptance. Either way, I love God so much, like the way I remembered when I was young, but in a more grown-up way.

What happened next is true and shows nothing but God's grace all the way to His glory; it speaks of his quiet and tender love for those whose hearts search for Him, in victory or defeat.

A sports reporter for our local newspaper had caught wind of the story about the two brothers. He had started following the team a bit. He said, "The team seemed special; they seemed close." They started winning games in district play that were heart-throbbers.

They began to play like it was destiny, winning every game in the last inning, four or five of them with clutch hits from Tennyson. The first game of William's return, he went 2 for 4 with four RBIs and a homerun. Tennyson hit a homerun in the same game, fulfilling the dream from a late night talk, hoping they could homer in the same game.

More and more people came to the games. A lot of people remembered last year's loss in the state sectional. A lot of people were there to see their boys or to be with friends or friends' parents. Some were there just to watch baseball. Some were there for all that and to remember their lives and to see what God would do. Some hoped like children in a tragic world to see a glimpse of grandeur.

The newspaper reporter, Roger Garfield, wrote a story about Tennyson, William, hopes, dreams, dedication, and destiny. It was titled, "Brotherly Destiny," and a piece of the article reads as follows:

> Whatever sacrifices he had to make, however many extra hours he would have to spend in the batting cage, William Dodd was prepared to do it for his brother.
>
> It began with a promise.
>
> The day after Oakland's crushing loss to Cleve-

land in last year's Class AAA state sectional, William told his brother, Tennyson, that he would be back—that, no matter what, Tennyson would get a shot at redemption his senior year.

I said, 'Tennyson, I'll do anything,' says William, a sophomore.

'I'll work as hard as you want me to work. Use me. Teach me what you do, and I'll do anything you want me to do to get you back.'
(*Daily News Journal*, Tuesday, May 20, 2008, C1)

Tennyson told the reporter that he and William worked together every day. They hit and they conditioned. He said that he had never been more proud of his brother in his whole life. "He could have easily been done for the season, but he worked hard and got back." To see him go through these hard things, come back, and do "what he talked about doing when he was sitting on the bench has been amazing."

William said, " I knew how hard Tennyson had worked. He had given himself to baseball completely, and it didn't turn out the way he wanted it to turn out."

It had not turned out the way either one of them had dreamed until a Friday night in the bottom of the ninth inning with the game tied 4 to 4 in the very same game the team lost the year before. William had helped his brother return. William and Tennyson had been together step for step.

Of all possibilities that could have occurred, Tennyson came to the plate. He had two balls and two strikes, two innings into extra innings.

William's dream had become a living truth: "I'll do whatever it takes to get back to that game, so you can finish what you didn't get to finish." The pitch is thrown, Tennyson hits a towering fly ball to right field; a combined silence of hopes in held breath waited to exhale in celebration. The outfielder runs back until his hand is on the right-field wall, and the ball sails over the fence into the dark. Tennyson had rounded first before everyone realized what had happened. The crowd erupted with joy. I remember the fist pumping joy and breathless sense of painful wonder on Tennyson's face as he rounded first base. And I remember William was the first player to meet him at home plate, jumping and fist pumping until the whole team piled up at home plate with William and Tennyson on the bottom together. I asked them later what it was like being on the bottom of a celebration pile. They said it was the best hurt they had ever felt.

What made the home run so beautiful was the improbability of the underneath story of heart punching through reality. Not the home run so much, as the desire of heart developing, being stated, walked towards, and coming true. A younger brother dreams with an older brother. They even pray together. Love overcomes what could have been a typical, calloused, surface relationship with daily living. Passion, healing, courage, forgiveness, freedom, humility, acceptance, intimacy, faith, and joy won.

Those moments were the second most beautiful scene I have ever touched, and they were made of years.

The first most beautiful scene I have ever touched followed that night.

The team made it to the state playoffs, lost the first game, won the second with late game heroics. The third game they were eliminated. The team left seventeen runners on base and lost by a 3-2 score. That loss and believing hearts propelled beauty that summer night. It was the perfect loss.

All the players slowly walked to left field, most crying about a hard fought game, loss, dreams, mistakes, some because this game was the last time they would ever play together; some of them had played together since they were seven years old. My own sons' time to play together was over.

This time the game ended again with a last strikeout. The beauty began at that moment. Heart and love ruled that night. When the player struck out, Tennyson ran from first base to home plate, and William ran from the dugout to home plate to console a brokenhearted friend. They all had dreamed like us of victory, celebration, and achievement that remains a smiling memory when young men's hair turns gray. Instead, a young man's shoulders were bent and tears flowed freely from a bowed head as he slowly removed his batting gloves.

The scene was captured by a photographer with a special eye. Tennyson had his hand on Phillip's bowed head and

William's hands were on his shoulders. Each man shed tears of hopes and dreams finally ended. They stood together in pain. Then they moved together to congratulate the winning team in baseball tradition.

With two other Dads, I walked around the clubhouse to the field gate at the third base line and our dugout. We sat inside the field on a brick wall to wait and wonder. I turned to my right, looked behind me into the shadows by the clubhouse and stared straight into the eyes of the young man who struck out in last year's sub-state game. I stood up and walked to him. He stood very still until I said, "Come on, they need you. You know what they are going through." He nodded and said, "I do." Then I spontaneously hugged him, and he began to weep hard. He was trying to say, "I know what it's like," through choking tears. He then walked out to where his old teammates were standing and kneeling out in left field.

The place was silent except for the buzzing that came from lights on the field and traffic sounds in the distance. About one hundred and fifty fans stood where they had been at game's end, waiting for something. I waved to one of them to come around. Sonya saw me and knew. She spoke to others to go. Slowly, every fan quietly came through the gate and onto the field to wait for this wonderful bunch of brave-hearted young men to come toward them. We all waited quietly, looking out to left field.

The pitching coach told me later that he was talking to the team, telling them how proud he was of them. As he finished, he turned to see a crowd of people waiting on the field. He said, "It was like a thing, like a town." He said, "When I saw all of you waiting, I lost it."

As the boys moved our way, a slow rising applause came up through the crowd and people were saying, "Thank you." As they got to us, parents and friends hugged their sons and friends. Everything that night was finished on the field; tears, smiles, stories, and goodbyes. Sonya and I hugged both of our sons. I hugged all the boys, and told them how I admired their fight. Other fathers, grandparents, and mothers hugged the players they had been watching for years and loving for years.

I watched Tennyson and another young man who he had played with since the first grade look at each other and start weeping about all the times of sweat, and their last time on a beautiful field of dreams on a perfect summer night. We walked off the field reconciled, knowing that a piece of heaven lives on earth everywhere if we see, and that we, no doubt, are a long way from heaven. We live fully now, and love deeply, and then lead well here, and yet we wait for the tragedy to end when we finally get there. My sons had believed, and on this night anyone who had eyes of the heart to see did see and believe.

A week later, Sonya pulled up to our home and found a large box gift-wrapped sitting by our mailbox. The box was wrapped in gift paper that had baseball players all over it. The only markings on the outside were "To Tennyson and William" written in magic marker. Inside were two plaques that had the article about their dreams reprinted from the newspaper. The gifts were such an honor. Even more so, though, the gifts were anonymous. A piece of paper in the box in typed letters read: "To two brothers who are a credit to each other, a joy to their family, and a point of pride for their community." I am still so honored to have had the chance to read that piece of paper from someone who saw what happened and believed and gave. Heart won and some loving person who was touched, touched back. Life is not a game. It is a war of love. The Beattitudes are true. They live if we live them.

The righteous keep finding God in the deep depths of themselves and all around them, and they cannot let go of Him. They fight for truth in a war of love; they fight for truth to overwhelm reality. Of course there is persecution, the move to silence love, for all power that does not surrender to love despises the believing heart. Sons and daughters of the believing heart are emissaries of a great and ancient King— our King. The King of kings and Lord of lords lives now with us and will return in full.

A day is coming when we all will see. Until then, I pray that faith, hope, and love grace each of us who believe, and that we will offer the peace of Jesus' passion to those who are yet to believe again—like when they were little.

EPILOGUE

———————

Almost a year has passed since that night on the baseball field. Tennyson went off to college, continuing to play the game he loves and struggling as a freshman. William is in the process of missing a second baseball season related to back problems. A spinal cord tumor was detected in late November. He underwent five hours of surgery after Christmas to remove the tumor; it was an invasive, delicate, and dangerous operation. The tumor was discovered in the midst of attempting to diagnose and repair lower back pain. Family and friends prayed with us and with William and attended to us throughout the process.

The tumor grew against the spinal cord in the spinal column. William wonders aloud and is struggling with the questions of life, and I pray that he stays in the struggle, not resigning his heart to gravity. When he came out of surgery, the recovery nurse told us that the first question he asked was, "How's my Mom?" I suspect the last thing he heard before they took him into their hands was Sonya's quiet, deep groan as her child was rolled away from her. We were

———————

270

left completely, utterly without illusion of control but for heart's desire and prayer.

Seven hours after surgery began, we were able to tell William that the surgeon said the tumor removal went as good as it could possibly go. The benign tumor separated beautifully from the spinal cord. He shut his eyes, breathed in, and then exhaled as tears began to roll down each side of his face. He said quietly, "Oh, good; thank God." He had been really scared. Me too. Our hearts are alive.

Two days ago an F-5 tornado hit our community. It stayed on the ground for twenty-two minutes deforming creation. Over one hundred homes were devastated. After it ended, the check for casualties began immediately. Then over the next two days of Easter weekend, several thousand people of all backgrounds went to work to assist the ones who had been hit. We all chopped, cut, sawed, hauled, gathered, fed, watered, sheltered, and clothed with a heart of empathy and courage. People, houses, and trees had been pulled from their roots and thrown into chaos.

Two of William's teammates' houses had been hit. His baseball team went out to move debris. William used the word devastation to describe what he saw. He said they threw everything that had been scattered everywhere into trucks to haul to construction dumpsters, including family photos and pictures of children.

The Beatitudes began again in this tragic life in which our God is faithful.

"Blessed are the poor in spirit, for theirs is the kingdom of heaven" is the beginning of living fully, loving deeply, and leading well. Light pierces darkness, hope overcomes despair, creation pushes through destruction, and courage beats death. We, the reconciled, live in surrender and find our strength in our Intimate Creator. We can say in the midst of all of life with surrendered hearts the truth:

> Though the fig tree does not bud and there are no grapes on the vines, though the olive crop fails and the fields produce no food, though there are no sheep in the pen and no cattle in the stalls, yet I will rejoice in the LORD. I will be joyful in God my Savior. The Sovereign LORD is my strength; he makes my feet like the feet of a deer, he enables me to go on the heights. (Habakkuk 3:17-19)

Let us stand on the ramparts watching for and being in what God is doing. Here am I, LORD, do with me what You will.

ACKNOWLEDGEMENTS

No one can succeed alone, and this work is no exception. I thank God for the following people who have been instrumental in joining me to place this book in your hands: To Phil Herndon and Stephen James, my friends who have unswervingly pushed me to produce. To Adria Haley who edited the work several times through before she was satisfied. To Mary Hooper who has the eye that produced the front cover and who gives her time because she believes in what we are doing at Sage Hill Resources. I also wish to thank Sonya and our sons whom I love, and my parents who have supported this work of redemption for the sake of love.

The
VOICE
of the
HEART

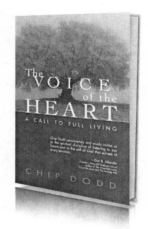

A CALL TO FULL LIVING

"Dodd passionately invites us to the spiritual discipline of listening to our hearts and to the call of God."

-- DAN B. ALLENDER, author of *The Wounded Heart, Cry of the Soul,* and *The Healing Path*

"Dodd reveals how our spiritual heart functions and how we can discover more of the life that Christ offers."

-- FRANKLIN GRAHAM

Profoundly insightful, *The Voice of the Heart* offers a deeper understanding of how to live an abundant life. Chip Dodd teaches us how to begin to know our hearts so that we better know ourselves and are better equipped to live in relationship with others and, ultimately, with God. Included with the book is a audio compact disc. The CD is a companion presentation by Chip Dodd to supplement the material covered in the book. It provides additional teaching on the Spiritual Root System, particularly how feelings play a vital role in our emotional and spiritual maturity.

www.sagehillresources.com

– Feelings Needs Desires Longings Hope –

SAGE HILL INSTITUTE
JER. 17:7-8

SAGE HILL INSTITUTE is a non-profit, Christ-centered, teaching and equipping organization dedicated to helping leaders be who they are made to be, so that they can do what they are made to do.

SHI is dedicated to do whatever is possible to help leaders articulate, implement, and fulfill their visions by helping them lead from their hearts with passion, intimacy, and integrity.

TEACHING/TRAINING

Through speaking, workshops, retreats, and conferences, we partner with organizations to instruct, equip, inspire, and encourage their staff and constituencies toward becoming more of who they desire to become.

LEADERSHIP & ORGANIZATIONAL CONSULTING

At the heart of every organization is it's people. Using the Spiritual Roots System, a way to understand how people are created, SHI works with leaders to help assess, develop, and implement strategies and programs that assist their organizations from a variety of perspectives, including:

- Leadership Consulting
- Executive Coaching
- Crisis Management
- Change Management
- Corporate Culture Reorganizing
- Strategic Planning
- Team Building

sagehillinstitute.org

CPSIA information can be obtained
at www.ICGtesting.com
Printed in the USA
LVOW08s0520310817
546964LV00001B/119/P